WHAT THEY S

Wealth Within Your Reach
Pera Mo, Palaguin Mo!

Going back to the basics of personal financing has never been as fun. Mr. Colayco manages to chat his readers into an otherwise difficult journey of self-discovery with his delightful insights on the very serious subject of money.

ZORAYDA AMELIA C. ALONZO
Chairman & CEO, Small Business Guarantee Finance Corporation

The book's main message is clear and simple: financial independence is within the reach of anyone, even those who struggle with economic difficulties. Readers will walk away from this book with ideas and tools that can be used immediately. I highly recommend it.

Fr. GREGG L. BANAGA, Jr., CM
President, Adamson University

This book fills a need that has always been there but has not been really paid much attention to. As it seeks to inform, it also inspires, encourages and gives hope. A copy of this book in one's library will not only be useful to its owner but can be handed on from generation to generation.

Atty. FE B. BARIN
Member, Monetary Board, Bangko Sentral ng Pilipinas

In my work with the Bishops'-Businessmen's Council as Co-Chairman of the Committee on Labor and Employment, I have long felt the need for a financial planning guide for our friends in the informal sector and the OFWs. I strongly recommend that financial planning be undertaken from the start. The ideas and suggestions in this book are easy to understand and apply in one's livelihood and family life.

MENELEO J. CARLOS, Jr.
President, Resins, Inc. & Chairman, Federation of Philippine Industries

This is a very well-written, well-thought-out book on money matters. Filled with simple yet practical ideas, it makes for easy reading. Two years worth of graduate school level material is condensed into one volume.

MARIA TERESA L. CHAN
President & CEO, A.C. Steel Industries Inc. and Sugarsteel Industries Inc.

What I like most about the book is the way it is presented in layman's terms. I intend to give copies to my wife, my children and relatives. I find in this book all the financial concepts that I want to relay and express to my loved ones but could not do so because of time constraints and shortness of patience to express these concepts in a language understandable to everyone.

ALFONSO B. CRUZ, JR.
Executive Vice-President, Land Bank of the Philippines

I enjoyed reading this book. As someone who has been dealing with overseas Filipinos for some 25 years now in various parts of the globe, I know that many of them are in need of the concepts and tips provided. It's truly the kind of advice they have long been waiting for.

JOSE VICENTE CUIZON
Executive Vice President & Special Assistant to the President, Philippine National Bank

The book is truly educational and enriching presenting complex fundamentals of money, finance and investments into easily understandable and fun to read teachings. It provides as well an invaluable bonus as it relives, refreshes and inculcates the readers with time honored values such as industry, honesty, diligence, temperance and many other values for one to live a full, meaningful and decent life.

ROBERTO JUANCHITO T. DISPO
Executive Vice President, First Metro Investment Corporation
Former Deputy National Treasurer of the Philippines

The author uses simple, straightforward talk. Shifting effortlessly from English to Pilipino, he puts finance in a much simpler light, very understandable to the OFWs who can develop a culture of entrepreneurship in our country. Mr. Colayco's book could just open doors towards our dream of a prosperous nation of entrepreneurs. I am glad to find in him a kindred soul.

Dr. ROLANDO HORTALEZA
Founder and Chairman, Splash Corporation

This book certainly meets a very important need of OFWs, ordinary employees and small business owners. It is comprehensive and covers everything a person wants to know about savings, investments, loans and how to gain wealth, manage it and make it grow.

REMEDIOS L. MACALINGCAG
Former President, Development Bank of the Philippines

Because the book is written in simple language, interspersed with true-to-life stories, the reader will find it easy to read and interesting. Congratulations for an excellent work!

VICTOR MACALINGCAG
Former National Treasurer and Undersecretary of Finance of the Philippines

Every income-earner who seeks financial independence is an entrepreneur. This book effectively provides the tools for everyone, particularly OFWs who are the real players in the globalization of the workplace, to achieve their financial stability. As an educator, I endorse this book as a must reading not only for income-earners and OFWs, but more importantly, for all students. Those who are in training and education must promote this advocacy.

AMELOU BENITEZ-REYES, Ph.D.
President, Philippine Women's University

This book is not only for OFWs but also for ALL Filipinos - for expatriates, professionals, lawyers, doctors, housewives, etc. It has the gift of encouraging the reader to read further as there is so much initial interest awakened.

Justice ANDRES B. REYES, Jr.
Associate Justice, Court of Appeals

This book is a noble work, written to motivate ordinary workers to realize that they can build a future. Mr. Colayco has made the journey toward wealth creation doable and attainable to his target audience. It is delightful reading even for those like me who have spent a lifetime in the financial services industry.

EVELYN R. SINGSON
President, eBusiness Services Inc. (eBiz)

MORE ON WHAT THEY SAY ABOUT

WEALTH WITHIN YOUR REACH
PERA MO, PALAGUIN MO!

"A "must-read" for everyone who, in spite of age or other sophistications, is still undisciplined or clueless about personal finance."

Dr. Lydia B. Echauz
President, Far Eastern University
Philippines

"...As Chairman and Vice Chair respectively of the Committee on Education and Committee on Livelihood and Employment of the Sectoral Council, I am persuaded that Mr. Colayco can be helpful in the quest of the Filipino PWDs to be self reliant...."

Lauro L. Purcil Jr.
Sector of Persons with Disabilities (PWD) of
The National Anti Poverty Commission (NAPC)

"...i'm really thanking you dahil sa pag introduce nyo po dito sa ksk program. ang tanong ko po [BAKIT NGAYON LANG KAYO?]...speaking of the book nag text ako sa pinas to introduce to them too, dahil gusto ko pati din sila doon aware anong dapat gagawin sa perang kinita..."

SYLVIA of HONG KONG

"...the book is really very informative & I learned a lot. I will apply it in my life & share also to my brothers & friends. [FJC] is one among God's messenger to share his knowledge & I am inspired to strive more in order to have a FINANCIAL INDEPENDENCE soon!!!..."

Teresa Saradolla
OFW in Hong Kong

"...For me, Mr. Colayco's book, as most of us are in a jungle of poverty is a guide, a map, a compass to escape from it, it's now all up to us to make a single step for a long lasting journey towards a brighter future..."

Elena V. Salado
OFW in Hong Kong

"...para sa akin this is the moment na umpisa na ng pag-ahon sa kalayaan sa kakapusan... Actually,di naman sa pagbubuhat ng sariling bangko im already in the build -up phase kaya lang ngayon ko lang nalaman na sa inyo na marami palang instrumento na pwede naman hindi na kami pabalik-balik dito sa abroad..."

Yolanda Panong
OFW in Hong Kong

"I would like to order the book on KSK. Everybody is telling that it's really great so i would like to order and could apply it to myself too..."

Marilou Baniaga

OFW in Hong Kong

"... I would like to express my warmest thanks for teaching me personal finance and how could attain financial independence...May GOD bless you and ksk coop be successful for the benefit of us ofw and others keep up the GOODWORK..."

Petty Angoluan
OFW in Hong Kong

EVEN MORE ON WHAT THEY SAY ABOUT:

WEALTH WITHIN YOUR REACH
PERA MO, PALAGUIN MO!

This book is very timely, relevant and useful especially at a time of financial crisis. Francisco Colayco is a true winner . . . he showed genuine concern to his readers by providing them the *WAY* and the *WILL* to financial independence. Anyone who is really serious in having a blueprint to personal wealth should have his book.

RADM Danilo A. Abinoja
Deputy Commandant for Operations
Philippine Coast Guard

". . .I proudly admit that this book of Topax Colayco is the only one that I have ever bought 60 copies of and, have given away 59 of them. The single copy I kept for myself, has even made the rounds in my household. I will not repeat the contents nor would I dare to re-state his creative explanations in my words – that would be presumptious – but, I must use the oft repeated phrase of book reviews, THIS IS A MUST READ! And add, THIS IS A MUST BUY AND A MUST GIVE AWAY!

. . . complex terms and ideas in the business scene, when creatively reduced into layman's language, will get the layman's attention and support. More importantly, when the man-in-the-street understands what he reads, he inevitably enriches himself. And, when he is enriched, a whole country is enriched in the process. God knows our country needs all the enriching it can get."

Jesus Martinez
Commissioner, Securities and Exchange Commission

Mr Colayco has explicitly put into words everything I have been wanting to articulate to my children regarding financial management. This book is indeed a legacy I have been dreaming to pass on. And I just did.

Jimmy Gomez,
President, Fat Jimmy Resort, Boracay

This book taught me what I did not learn in medical school. It was like an examination of conscience on how I dealt with my finances in the past and for penance, I resolve to seriously manage it by applying the simple but basic principles outlined in this book and to spread the good news to all.

Cynthia B. Gomez, M.D.
Pediatrician, The Medical City

"I have just purchased your book and would like to thank you for this wonderful knowledge you have imparted to me and my family. You mixed education, reality and fun so well."

Oscar Ryan Santillan
Davao City

"All I've learned and read from your book, I have started to share with my family. I asked them to buy it and read. Also, I have also recommended and shared your book with my co-workers."

Cesar Ramirez
OFW Saudi Arabia

"I have read your book and was inspired by it. As you've said it's never too late for us to learn to handle our personal finances."

Jojo U. Fong

"Kudos to your new book Mr. Colayco, truly an enlightening and the best book so far on personal financial management."

Rizal Gonzales

"I know your book is not to teach people para magmukhang pera kundi para turuan ang mga tao na pahalagahan ang biyayang kanilang natanggap at gamitin sa tamang paraan. Sana po hindi man yumaman ang mga Pilipino, matuto man lang mamuhay ng maayos, malinis, kapakipakinabang at may karangalan sa pamamagitan ng inyong libro at mga seminar."

Jocelyn Miranda
OFW-Japan

. . .maraming salamat po sa pagkasulat niyo ng malaman na aklat na ito. Matatapos ko na po ang aklat marahil sa loob ng 2 araw. Nguni't balak ko na basahin pa itong muli ng paulit-ulit upang maisapuso ko ang lahat ng konsepto at prinsipyo na itinuturo niyo sa inyong aklat.. .

Robert D. Guinto
High School Teacher

(Author's note: My sincere gratitude to Mr. Guinto who contributed to our advocacy by improving the Tagalog/Pilipino portions in the Sixth printing.)

Wealth Within Your Reach

Pera Mo, Palaguin Mo!

Wealth Within Your Reach
Pera Mo, Palaguin Mo!

Published by
Colayco Foundation for Education, Inc.
Telephone nos.: 637-3741, 631-4446, 63-917-853-7333
Fax no.: 637-3731
Email address: info@colaycofoundation.com
www.colaycofoundation.com

Distributed by
Anvil Publishing, Inc.
(Megastrat, Inc.)
8007-B Pioneer St., Bgy. Kapitolyo, Pasig City 1603 Philippines
Tels.: 637-5141, 637-3621, 631-7045
Fax: 637-6084
Website: www.anvilpublishing.com

Editor
MONINA ALLAREY MERCADO

Text Editors
BOOTS RUELOS & MARIA SILAYAN

Cover Design by
INA COLAYCO-BAUTISTA of IN.C Design Studio

Cover Photo taken by
MANDY NAVASERO

Book Design by
TEODY V. HIDALGO

Illustrations by
MIKE DE PERALTA
Kateods

ISBN 971-92995-0-9

Printed in the Philippines
Five Printings for 2004
Three Printings for 2005
Three Printings for 2006
Twelfth Printing - January 2007
Printed by COR-Asia, Inc.

Wealth
Within Your
Reach

PERA MO, PALAGUIN MO!

BY

Francisco J. Colayco

.

To my wife, Mary Anne, who has been most supportive in creating a truly meaningful life for me. To her and the other three women in my life, my children Cessie, Ina and Lia, my love and gratitude. Without their unceasing influence and affection, I would not have had the motivation to achieve our own Kalayaan sa Kakapusan.

This book is dedicated to every income-earning Filipino who constantly faces the challenge of providing for his family's financial needs. Clearly set forth here are the principles and tools, which if understood and utilized early in life, would serve to ease the journey towards financial independence.

In particular, this book is dedicated to the millions of Overseas Filipino Workers. Known as the OFWs, they are a special group who make the supreme sacrifice of leaving their families to earn a living in distant shores. They are the new heroes of the Philippine Economy. They bring in the needed foreign exchange to boost the economy.

Many OFWs come back with hardly enough money to retire comfortably after their many years of hardship. Worse, they end up with just the same or even less than what they had when they first left. Many have perhaps been mistreated and many more have been ill advised particularly with regard to the money they have earned.

With this book and our seminars, I hope to be able to help them move towards their own financial independence: *Kalayaan sa Kakapusan!*

Table of Contents

4

FOREWORD

I HAVE ALWAYS believed in sharing. Sharing thoughts, experiences, discoveries, news. In fact, there is something especially gratifying in sharing good news. And because of this, I feel strongly that I would now like to share certain principles in personal finance that have proven invaluable in growing and ensuring my financial well being. My advocacy started this way.

One night, while driving home and listening to the radio, I came across the show of a woman selling her own brand of nutritional supplements. She lured listeners with the promise that they could earn substantial sums of money by selling her product. From the number of callers, it was evident that her show enjoyed quite a following.

At that time, I was deeply involved in advising sales agents and marketers on the management of their growing personal earnings.

Then it hit me. What if I start a radio show that would spread the news that financial independence is within everyone's reach? What if I tell them that all they need to do is to prepare and acquire the ability to reach it? I could focus on teaching people how to manage their earnings. I certainly would be able to reach out to more people and not limit myself to marketers and sales agents. I could, in fact, reach out to all who are gainfully employed, particularly the Overseas Filipino Workers (OFWs).

But then, I asked myself, what do I have to offer really?

Looking back, I realized that my background is no different from that of the great majority of Filipinos, who have to start without any real funds to invest.

I was born during the last stages of World War II. My father was killed when I was only four months old. My mother was a teacher. She was left with seven children and the eldest was only ten years old.

Against terrific odds, my mother managed to get all of us educated. Perhaps it was because my father, Manuel, Sr. was a war hero and my mother, Clemencia was a teacher that many people went out of their way to help. Nonetheless, I know it took a lot of sacrifice and hardship on my mother's part.

I was a professional manager for almost 20 years. I started as a management trainee in Procter & Gamble in 1965 and worked with the company for two years. Thereafter, I went through two years of a full-time master's course in business management and then engaged in project management and management consultancy with Asia's largest accounting and management services firm.

In the next decade, I managed and developed a local construction and shipbuilding company and brought the company to the Middle East, making it the first Filipino service contractor in the region. In my last four years of employment, I headed the international operations of the largest Filipino conglomerate at that time.

In 1984, at the age of 40, I became an entrepreneur. In partnership with French and Swiss firms, I established an engineering and operations management company that engaged in service contracting overseas. This was a field of endeavor we all knew by heart. Collectively, we had over 40 years of field experience. We had secured seven signed contracts even before our company was fully organized. With these seven contracts we were assured of continuous and profitable operations for at least three years. The opportunity we had, and the situation we worked our way to, was the envy of would-be entrepreneurs. Alas, as fate would have it, none of our signed contracts ever materialized.

Pero kung hindi ukol, hindi bubukol! Wala ni isa sa pitong pirmadong kontrata ang natuloy. Halos maubos ang aming kapital sa kahihintay sa pagsulong ng mga kontratang yoon. Ang sabi nga nila, walang siguradong negosyo kundi yung negosyong nagpapasok na ng salapi sa bulsa mo. Bagamat ang pirmadong kontrata ay mahalaga at kadalasan ay sapat na para paglagakan ng pawis at salapi, hindi pa rin ito dapat tanggapin na 100% na katiyakan.

My partners and I were not discouraged. We set out and booked new contracts with European and Japanese clients we had worked with in the past. The contracts were not as profitable, but they kept the company going. Eventually, as the Middle East markets declined, we decided to end the joint venture, and subsequently, I closed the company. It was a slight financial failure. But it was a resounding success in entrepreneurial learning and international exposure.

From there, with the backing of financial investors, I moved on to real estate development in San Francisco. We acquired a historical building to develop as a modern apartment hotel. We had solid financial plans with firm and substantial cash equity pledges. The big earthquake of 1988 came just as we were making the call for the second round of cash capital that was earlier pledged. Understandably, the concerned investors backed out. The earthquake killed the real estate market and eventually that venture. Our investments got wiped out.

With some of the same investors' backing and with bank loans, I moved on to several real estate development projects in Manila. This time, all of them were successful and our previous losses were recovered.

Mabuti na lang at hindi nawala ang tiwala sa akin ng mga investor at bangko. Sa tingin ko, ito ay dahil sa tulong ng poong Maykapal at sa aking pagiging tapat sa kanila. Alam din nila na bagamat nabigo ang aming pamumuhunan, ang desisyon nilang maglagak ng kanilang salapi ay batay sa isang masusing pagsusuri. Alam din nila na hinarap ko sila nang mahusay sa hirap at ginhawa.

Paulit-ulit sa buhay ko ang leksiyon na dapat tayong humarap nang mahusay sa lahat ng ating katrato sa lahat ng panahon, maginhawa man o mahirap.

It was in 1990 that my partners and I bought Professional Academic Plans, Inc. and Professional Pension Plans, Inc., which later became The Professional Group. (TPG). From a relatively small company we grew to almost seven times in size in less than four years. It was becoming clear then that the pre-need industry was growing fast and that it needed bigger and more structured funding resources. In 1995, an Indonesian conglomerate bought the company and made it a condition that I stay on as president. Again, as fate would have it, in 1997, the Asian financial crisis struck. The Indonesian conglomerate suffered massive financial losses. This led to heavy negative publicity about the Indonesian TPG. To maintain market share in 1998, I arranged for transitional ownership of the company with the assistance of a financial institution. A year later, a new set of financial investors acquired control of the company now known as Professional Financial Plans.

These experiences have taught me valuable lessons in handling corporate and personal finances.

Bukod sa aking mga karanasan sa personal finance, ang aking natutunan sa corporate finance ay isinalin ko sa mga personal na alintuntuning pinansyal.

Through this book, I wish to share with you some of these lessons. It is my hope that by learning from, and practicing the financial principles and experiences I have lived by throughout most of the last 25 years, you too will be able to achieve financial freedom.

Ang hangad ko ay magamit ninyo ang aking mga karanasan upang maisagawa ninyo ang maayos na palatuntunan na makapagdudulot ng kasaganaang pinansyal sa inyong kabuhayan.

My desire to reach out led me to get on the AM radio band and talk about ***"Usapang Kabuhayan"*** and, eventually, a fateful encounter with the leaders of the Confederation of Overseas Filipino Workers in Hong Kong (COFW). This brought about the simulcast of the long-time running and very successful "Philippines Tonight Show" radio program in Hong Kong and the Philippines. As co-host with the program founders, Michael Vincent Benares and "Tita Keri" (Federico "Jun" Paragas), we continue to reach out every week to share the principles of personal finance with OFWs and their families.

Kalayaan sa Kakapusan

Kalayaan sa Kakapusan or KsK, as an arm of the Colayco Foundation for Education, was a corporate mission that has become my personal advocacy. Over the past two years, our radio program has reached out to thousands of OFWs, ordinary employees, and small business owners who are eager to learn how they can keep and grow the money that they are currently earning.

On November 9, 2003, KsK held the first Personal Finance Seminar in Hong Kong. Around 400 OFWs attended. The seminar taught them the basic principles of financial freedom, or freedom from want.

On March 28, 2004, the second Personal Finance Seminar was held in Hong Kong. Again, around 400 OFWs attended. Aside from the subject matter of the first seminar, we also explained the concept of Cooperatives.

Through these seminars, they became aware that every single person or family, rich or poor, goes through stages of financial needs. They learned that proper management of personal finance must take this into account. The seminar explained the fundamental rules of wealth generation, income, and debt management.

This book is an offshoot of those seminars and the "Philippines Tonight Show" radio program. Through this book I hope to encourage the average Filipino worker, people like the OFWs who listen to our radio program every week.

My main message: financial independence is within your reach. If, today, you are able to generate income, you have the capital and you can grow it! But you must act NOW!

Ang aking mensahe ay "Kaya mong maging malaya sa kakapusan". kung ikaw ay kumikita, mayroon kang pagkukuhanan ng puhunan at ito ay kaya mong palaguin. kailangan lang ay mag-umpisa ka na agad!

This book will demonstrate the means to achieve KsK that are available to anyone who is willing to learn and avail of them. I want to assure you that the required tasks are not at all difficult, that all it takes is your commitment to learn to save and provide for your future. This book is the first in a series that will explain the fundamental rules of wealth generation, income and debt management.

People need to be aware that they have to prepare for their personal and family's financial future. Achieving financial well being is not an option. It is an obligation. I hope that in some way, this book will help to fulfill that obligation.

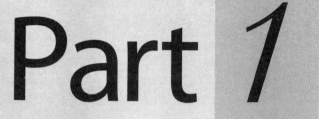
Part 1

Where You Are

CHAPTER 1

A success story that became a sad story

Success, failure, success again---
this can be your story, too.

AT THE AGE of 32, PJ became a very successful marketer since he was a very driven and hardworking man.

PJ was born in an impoverished town in Davao. Because his family was very poor, he learned to fend for himself at an early age. By the time he was eight years old, he was already working. He did all sorts of odd jobs, from tending pigs and chickens to becoming a laborer at a mining firm. But despite all the hardships he went through, he never stopped believing that one day he would succeed in life and would be able to rescue his family from poverty. This dream kept him from giving up.

At 18, after finishing high school, he decided to try his luck in Manila. Using money he won from a singing contest, he went to Manila with nothing but his burning desire to make it big someday. He promised himself that he would not set foot in his hometown again unless he was a millionaire.

In Manila, he worked as a helper at a small restaurant, as an opener and bagger at the post office, as a messenger, as a security guard, and even as a taxi driver. He took on two to three different jobs at the same time so he could start saving for his college education. At one point, he decided to sell small items to augment his income.

Once he started selling, he realized that he had a special gift. He found it easy to convince people to buy his wares. Around that time, the multi-level concept of marketing was starting to become popular. He figured it was just the type of business he was waiting for. He knew he would succeed. And succeed he did. He worked for several multi-level marketing firms. He finally hit it big, In February 2001, he joined a pioneering marketing group distributing financial and pre- need plans.

He was able to earn over fifteen million pesos (PhP 15,000,000) in just 18 months. His dream, apparently, had finally come true.

Mula sa karukhaan, si PJ ay naging multi-millionaire.
Success did not last long (biglang yaman na nawala)

Sadly, financial success is not the end of PJ's story. In less than two years he ended up losing most of the money he had earned.

Emboldened by his instant wealth, PJ began to indulge in unnecessary luxuries. A brand new Pajero was his first purchase. Next came the extensive remodeling of his family's rented apartment; expensive furniture, two more vehicles, millions "invested" in a pyramiding scam; a movie production that was never completed; and big loans to friends for projects that were not viable.

He spent a lot of money on things that were unnecessary and did not bring in any income at all. But the worst part is that he could have spent that money for assets that he really needed. He needed a house, yet he preferred to spend for improving a house he did not own. For just a little more, he could have acquired his own house and lot.

Mukhang nagrelax na lang siya at hindi na
nagtrabaho. Hindi man lang nilagak ang
salapi sa mga paraan na kumikita. Ang mas
masama, siya ay gumasta ng malaki sa
bahay na inuupahan lamang. Sana ay
bumili o nagpagawa siya ng bahay na
talagang kanya.

Now you may ask: How did he end up losing all that money, money that he worked so hard to earn, in such a short span of time? He beat all odds to earn that kind of money. Why did he not work as hard to keep it?

This is the same question I repeatedly asked myself after I realized that, like PJ, most of other successful marketers were also probably losing money they used to only dream of having.

I realized soon enough that they did not know how to handle their personal finances. While all of them were driven by the desire to earn money, it became evident that most, if not all of them, had no real understanding of how to keep and manage money. Except for a very select few, not a single one actually had a clear and specific idea of how much he or she wanted to earn and, FOR WHAT SPECIFIC PURPOSE. They simply wanted to earn and earn more!

Ang karamihan ay hindi marunong magkwenta
at mamahala ng kanilang pera. Ang gusto lang ay
kumita nang kumita. Hindi natin binibigyan
ng kaukulang pansin ang pagpaplano ng kinikita.

While observing them, I noticed a particularly common behavior. Most of them had an automatic change in lifestyle as soon as they got their first big paycheck.

Instant gratification is the "culprit".

Mukhang tayong lahat ay natutukso
sa madaliang gantimpala.

They also made investments (or at least what they thought were investments) without fully considering the attendant risks.

They took no effort to understand how those "investments" would impact on their financial future. They had no real appreciation of what they were risking versus the potential gains they were promised.

All of them simply believed that the promised financial gains were going to happen without knowing or understanding HOW those gains or profits were going to be made.

Madali silang naniwala na sila ay magiging mas mayaman kahit hindi nila naiintindihan kung anu-ano ang sapalaran at panganib na dala ng kanilang pamumuhunan.

With the way they were spending their money, it was as if the money were coming from a bottomless well that would never run dry.

Gumagasta sila na parang walang katapusan ang pagdating ng pera.

This observation seems applicable to most employees, especially overseas Filipino workers. It was certainly not their intention to lose their money. They were just unprepared for sudden abundance. They had no real appreciation of, and much less preparation for money management.

The collective experience of these marketers proves that there are as many challenges and difficulties to earning money as in keeping it.

Magkasing-hirap ang magtrabaho at kumita ng pera pangalagaan at palaguin ang perang kinita.

Because PJ and other marketers looked up to me as a mentor, I eventually found myself dispensing personal financial advice. I did what I could to help them because I did not want to see them succeed and then lose everything, just like PJ.

As a happy ending, PJ has gotten back on his feet and is on his way to increasing his income and building real assets. This time, he assures me that he is applying the rules that I have taught them and that are discussed in the following pages.

Nakatutuwa na si PJ ay hindi nawalan ng pag-asa. Siya ay hindi nasiraan ng loob at ngayon ay unti-unti nang bumabangon. Nangako siya na makikinig na siya sa tama at mabuting payo.

You can do it. *Kaya mo 'to!*

- Growing your money is just as important as earning it. It is your obligation to learn and develop skills to manage your earnings.

  Tandaan mo na ang matuto ng tamang pamamahala ng salapi ay isang tungkulin. Alamin mo na magkasing-halaga ang magpalago at kumita ng pera

- Work hard to earn money but be sure to have a plan to keep and grow it.

  Magsumikap ka sa paghahanapbuhay ngunit tiyakin mo na may plano ka kung papaano palalaguin ang kinita mo.

CHAPTER 2

Your Financial Life Stages

*Wealth is having the money
to fund your needs at any given time.*

WEALTH generation is a life-long process. It is something that is built over time. It is planned for, periodically adjusted and executed with a firm hand. It needs clarity of thought and vision. It needs you to be financially literate.

Paano ba maging "financially literate"? To many, financial literacy means that you have to be an accountant; to some, this means that you have to have a college degree in finance. This is not true!

To be financially literate, all you have to know and understand is what you want for yourself and how you will match your financial resources to meet your future wants. Wealth is nothing more than having the money to fund your particular needs at any given time. Below are the keys:

 Anticipate your future needs.
Alamin ang iyong pangangailangan sa hinaharap.

Plan to have the resources to meet your needs.
Paghandaan at alamin ang mga wastong paraan upang makamit ang perang sasagot sa iyong pangangailangan.

Understand how you can adjust your needs against the reality of your available resources.
Ibagay o baguhin ang iyong pangangailangan para sumang-ayon sa iyong kakayahan.

Ang susi sa pagkamaalam sa mga bagay pinansyal ay nasa pang-unawa na ang kasaganaan o kayamanan ay ang pagkakaroon ng salaping pangtustos sa mga pangangailangan sa oras ng pangangailangan. Isaloob natin na ang antas ng pangangailangan sa araw-araw ay ang magtatakda kung ano ang sapat na kayamanan para sa atin. Ang antas ng kayamanan ni Pedro ay iba sa antas ng kayamanan na magbibigay buhay kay Juan. Mahalagang isaisip na ang antas ng ating pangangailangan ay dapat ring ibagay sa ating kakayahan. Mamuhay ng nakabagay at alinsunod sa iyong kaya.

Knowing how much you need to be wealthy is the first step to financial freedom. To achieve this, you must understand, know and accept that:

> :Ǭ: Wealth does not necessarily mean having millions and millions of pesos. Being wealthy simply means having the financial resources to support your chosen lifestyle.

> :Ǭ: Anyone can plan to have and achieve enough wealth consistent with his or her chosen lifestyle.

All of us go through four fundamental financial life stages, namely: Start-up Stage, Build-up Stage, Fine-Tuning or Asset Allocation Stage and Retirement Stage.

Start-up Stage

This is when your only source of income is your salary or earnings provided by your active participation in terms of time and talent.

Lahat ng kita mo ay galing sa iyong sariling oras at pagod.

Build-up Stage

This is when you now have some income coming from savings and investments, which contribute about at least 20% of your total income.

Nagtatrabaho ka pa rin ngunit mga 20% ng iyong kita ay nanggagaling na sa interes ng iyong naipon o kita ng napamuhunang pera.

Asset Allocation Stage

This is when at least a good portion (30-60%) of your income is being provided by your savings and investments.

Nagtatrabaho ka pa rin ngunit 30-60% ng iyong kita ay nanggagaling sa interes ng iyong naipon o kita ng napamuhunang pera.

Retirement Stage

This is when the income from your savings and investments is your only source to support your living expenses.

Lahat ng pera mo ay nanggagaling na sa interes ng iyong naipon o kita ng iyong napamuhunang pera.

Our financial goals and tools to achieve those goals are unique to our current life stage. We must be able to match the tools we use with the goals of that life stage.

These tools are available to all of us. Given the time and knowledge of these financial tools and correctly using both, our accumulation of true and meaningful wealth is assured.

Ang "Life Stages" ay hindi hinahambing sa edad ng tao. Mayroong tao na bata pa ay nasa "Asset Allocation Stage" na at mayroon namang may katandaan na ngunit nasa "Start-up Stage" pa.

This book provides the fundamental principles and tools to guide the individual in organizing his financial life at the first stage - Start-up Stage. This foundation is so critical to planning the journey toward wealth and financial independence. Your success is assured if you embrace these principles and practice them.

You will encounter failures and disappointments, but don't give up. Failure is part of the process of achieving lasting success. In subsequent publications, I hope to share with you more tools, more guidelines and more real-life examples on what to do at the three other stages of your financial lives.

It is easier to earn money than to keep it. This book will show you how to keep it and grow it!

Mas madaling kumita ng pera
sa sariling sikap kaysa palaguin ito ng kusa.
Huwag kayong mabahala. Kaya niyo ito!

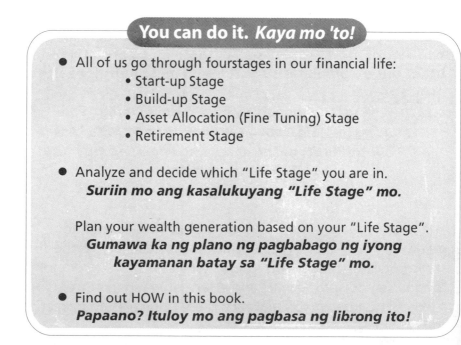

You can do it. *Kaya mo 'to!*

- All of us go through fourstages in our financial life:
  - Start-up Stage
  - Build-up Stage
  - Asset Allocation (Fine Tuning) Stage
  - Retirement Stage

- Analyze and decide which "Life Stage" you are in.
  Suriin mo ang kasalukuyang "Life Stage" mo.

  Plan your wealth generation based on your "Life Stage".
  Gumawa ka ng plano ng pagbabago ng iyong kayamanan batay sa "Life Stage" mo.

- Find out HOW in this book.
  Papaano? Ituloy mo ang pagbasa ng librong ito!

CHAPTER 3

Why You Need to Understand Personal Finance

Learn everything about your money.
Plan and monitor how it works for you.

FIFTEEN years ago, I entered the world of personal finance. Through my involvement in the pre-need industry, I became even more aware that the great majority focuses solely on earning money. So much effort and time are poured into this activity. Because of present needs, most people believe that earning money is one's primary goal, and earning more is the guaranty to happiness. Ironically, most people assume that once they have accumulated much money, they will never run out of it.

I realize that there really is not enough appreciation of the need to plan and set financial goals according to an individual's specific state of financial life. People do not seem to recognize that the more cash they have, the more problems they will face. Those who have come into sudden wealth would almost always end up with more financial problems.

If your problem is your inability to manage your earnings, no amount of earnings will solve your problem. The key to financial success lies in knowing:

- what your financial needs are;
- how to plan to meet those needs; and
- how to manage your earnings and expenses.

You need to be financially literate and you need to commit yourself to plan and monitor your financial progress.

So many have gone into business and continued to generate earnings for many years, only to one day end up with losses and debts far beyond what they ever earned. These are people who may have been doing well but simply did not have a true understanding of how to manage their personal versus business finances.

Marami sa atin ang nagnegosyo at kumita
sa mahabang panahon para lang umabot sa isang sitwasyon
na nawala lahat ang naipundar.

Di sana nangyari ito kung mayroon lang silang
sapat na pang-unawa sa tamang pamamahala ng pinansyal
personal at pinansyal pangkalakal o komersyal.

Hard work and a good track record of commercial success are not enough guarantees for financial success. Let me relate the story of Mrs. AC.

For almost 20 years (1974-1993), Mrs. AC engaged in wholesale distribution of food and commodities (rice, sugar, vinegar, etc.) to several barangays. Her daily sales were running at PhP 40,000. At the end of each month, after deducting ALL her expenses for costs of food supply and ALL OTHERS (including her household, personal and other payments for personal assets), she would still be left with around PhP 3,000.

Mrs. AC never paid herself any salary. She would just draw money from the business' cash flow for any need that she had, no matter whether it be for the business or for herself or her family. In the meantime, the business was doing well so Mrs. AC was able to acquire a jeep and four tricycles.

In 1993, Mrs. AC borrowed PhP 240,000 in order to finance her farmer suppliers so that she could be assured of cheaper supply. To get this loan, she had to mortgage her home, which the bank appraised at PhP 500,000. This plan did not work. The farmers could not pay her back.

Two major problems arose. Bad weather resulted in poor production, and she did not have the promised supply. In the meantime, she ran out of money to buy from others. Another more serious problem hit her too. Because of many factors beyond her control, the price of some of the commodities she had paid for in advance, dropped to less than half of her cost. She had to just forget about them, as it would have cost her more to physically gather them than to sell them at prevailing prices then.

In the meantime, Mrs. AC's business declined and closed down. Her original debt had by then gone up from PhP 240,000 to PhP 650,000. She had to sell all her assets. The bank foreclosed on her house, and she ended up still in debt. Today, Mrs. AC has gone back to employment and is now an OFW. Her husband passed away and the little insurance she received was used to reduce her outstanding debt.

Mrs. AC called me to relate her story so that others may learn from her mistakes. In listening to our radio program, she realized that she violated most of the success principles behind personal finance by:

- co-mingling her personal money requirements with the business funds;

- going into business operations (financing of commodity suppliers) in which she had no expertise;

- putting at risk a business that was doing well enough for a potentil gain that was not clearly defined; and

- failing to analyze and understand the business risks she took.

Tatlong isyu ang dapat bigyang pansin sa galaw ni Mrs. AC:

Unang-una, *hindi dapat paghaluin ang perang personal sa pera ng bisnes.*

Ikalawa, *hindi dapat pinasukan ni Mrs. AC ang supplier financing kung saan wala siyang sapat na kaalaman.*

Sa biglang tingin, para namang tama ang ginawa ni Mrs. AC. Gusto niyang gumanda ang kita niya kung mag "pre-pay" siya ng supply. Sa pagpauna ng bayad sa mga farmers, inakala ni Mrs. AC na naisiguro na niya ang presyo at pagkakaroon ng mga panindang kailangan niya. Di niya sinuring maigi ang mga panganib na pinasok sa hakbang na isinagawa niya.

Pangatlo, *kung dapat man, sa pangkaraniwan, hindi tama na gumamit ng utang para magpautang. Kung sakali man, ito ay dapat suriing maigi at timbangin ang peligro na papasukan.*

Common Money Mistakes People Make

Perhaps, we will all have a better appreciation of the need to understand personal finance by reliving real-life experiences relayed in a simple role-playing game.

In this game, you will be asked to make decisions.

You have two equally favorite uncles or **tiyuhin**. **Mahal mo silang pareho**. Both are just simple working-class guys. Both are not rich and don't own any business. Both are not finance or investment experts. But in your family, everyone seems to respect both of them. No one ever contradicts what either of them says. Maybe it's because they both really just happen to be nice persons. **Tatawagin natin silang Tiyo Andoy at Tiyo Inting**.

Let's also pretend that among their nephews and nieces, you are the favorite of both Tiyo Andoy and Tiyo Inting. And let's say you have PhP 500,000 in the bank that you can withdraw anytime. You earned that money by working as an OFW for a number of years. It is your life savings.

Scenario 1:

Let's pretend that I am your favorite Tiyo Andoy. I am with you now, sitting in a restaurant and I'm telling you, in between scoops of halo-halo, that I have a good friend who is very close to me. This friend has several successful businesses. But he has a problem. He badly needs cash to finance his latest business venture. This new business venture is guaranteed to generate a sizeable profit but, in the meantime, he needs cash so he could start it right away. If you "invest" your PhP 500,000 in his latest business venture, he will be paying you a monthly interest of 4%, or 48% per year. In one year, your PhP 500,000 will become PhP 740,000. There's just no other way you could earn that amount of money, I tell you. This is a sure deal, he is really a good friend of mine, and I try to convince you some more.

Will you invest your hard-earned money in the business of Tiyo Andoy's friend?

Scenario 2:

Now, let's pretend I am your favorite Tiyo Inting. We're sitting in another restaurant and I'm telling you, in between scoops of halo-halo: "Alam mo, I am planning to set up a small business. But I have a problem. I do not have enough cash to start my business. I know that you have managed to save Php 500,000 over the years. I am asking you to lend me your Php 500,000, and I am making a promise to pay you 2% per month and that I will be able to pay you everything (principal and interest) in one year."

Will you lend Tiyo Inting your life savings of PhP 500,000?

Based on my experience with my radio listeners and my continuing interaction with the general public, I would guess that most of you would answer YES to Tiyo Andoy , i.e., you would invest in the business of your uncle's friend; and NO to Tiyo Inting, i.e., you would not lend your savings to your uncle.

Marami sa atin ang naniniwala na kapag "investment," sigurado, pero kung pautang, delikado. Hindi natin napapansin kalimitan na ang salitang "invest" ay ginagamit kahit na ang tunay na layunin ay umutang.

Many people have the mistaken notion that "investments" are sure deals while loans are too risky. Consequently, they make the mistake of making hasty, and costly, investment decisions. They do not realize that when they are offered the opportunity

27

to invest in something, they are actually being asked, by whoever made that offer, to lend their money. They focus only on the promised rewards without adequate assessment of risks. Worse, they don't give due consideration to the credibility and capability of the one making the investment offer. Being a respected relative, a *"tiyahin o tiyuhin"* seems to be sufficient assurance of the soundness of the investment.

Chapter 17 discusses the differences between investment (equity or capital) and loans.

The Story of Mr. F & Mrs. G

Let me cite an actual example. Mr. F & Mrs. G are two very successful marketers. Mr. F is an engineer while Mrs. G is a midwife. They dreamt of succeeding financially, and through hard work and perseverance, they were able to do so.

But they had to go through a lot of difficulties before they achieved the financial freedom that they are enjoying now. They were professionals working in Saudi Arabia when they met. After they got married, they decided to return to the Philippines and set up a small business using the money they saved while working abroad.

They went into several businesses. Most of the time, they were just able to breakeven. There were even times when they lost money. But they never lost hope. They kept on looking for ways to earn money. They tried their hand at multi-level marketing too. It was then that they were finally able to succeed financially. They were earning a minimum of PhP 200,000 monthly. They were able to buy a nice house and lot, and a good car. In time, they were able to save too. It was when they had cash savings of PhP 700,000, back in 1998, that they met this lady whom we shall call Mrs. T.

Mrs. T was a good friend of their close and trusted friend, Mr. M. They considered Mr. M very trustworthy because they had dealt with him many times in the past. Shortly after they met, Mrs. T told them of her dilemma. She said that she was in the foreign exchange business and that she actually had a shop somewhere in Binondo.

She was in dire need of cash. In fact, she needed a few million pesos for the business. If Mr. F & Mrs. G could "invest" some money in her business she would pay them back at an interest rate of 30% a year. Because Mrs. T was a friend of their trusted friend Mr. M and because the interest earnings would be so high, they did not think twice about investing all their cash savings in her business. They did not even bother to check if her shop in Binondo really existed.

After they received the interest for the first month, Mrs. T told them that she needed more money for the business. Because they did not have more money to invest, Mr. F & Mrs. G proceeded to call and convince three of their friends to invest money in Mrs. T's business. They were able to solicit PhP 1.8 million, which they immediately gave to Mrs. T.

Within a couple of months, Mrs. T told them the sad news: her shop was robbed. The robbers took all the money. She promised she would do everything to pay them back. Then, she disappeared. Mr. F & Mrs. G did not only lose their savings of

PhP 700,000; they also ended up paying off the "investments" they solicited from their three friends.

The mistake that Mr. F & Mrs. G committed is just one of the most common money mistakes that people make, **Pinoys** in particular. It is a mistake that is obviously a result of misplaced trust and carelessness, perhaps influenced by greed. They were lured by the high interest rate even if they knew that very few legal businesses could offer that level of returns.

Sina Mr. F at Mrs. G ay kaagad nagbigay ng tiwala sa kaibigan ng matalik na kaibigan. Ito ay maitutulad sa tiyuhin na halimbawa natin kanina. Natukso rin sila sa mataas na interes kahit alam nila na ang mga lehitimong negosyo ay malabong makabayad ng ganoon kataas na interes.

Happily, Mr. F & Mrs. G have more than recovered from their early mistakes. They now have a clear financial plan that defines their objectives in terms of necessary assets (e.g. a bigger house for a growing family), earning assets and income and cash flow targets based on specific time schedules. Also, they now consult with appropriate professionals in refining and executing their personal financial program.

Bukod sa pagtitiwala sa mga kaibigan at tiyuhin, hindi sila dating kumukonsulta sa mga tunay na professional consultant. Hindi rin sila gumagawa ng masusing planong pinansyal. Ang mga desisyon nila ay hindi pinag-iisipan nang mabuti.

We don't make personal financial plans. Often, we make spur-of-the-moment spending decisions, without considering how these decisions would impact on our financial future.

Investments made without study nor purpose
(Paglagak ng salapi na walang pagsusuri)

I remember a listener of my radio program, Ms. B, who once called to ask me if she should sell or keep a piece of land that she bought somewhere in Cavite. I asked her what her objective was when she bought that land. She was not planning to use the land, it was just an investment, she said. She bought the land at PhP 2,000 per square meter. Today, she said, the selling price had gone up to PhP 3,500 per square meter. I told her it would be wise to sell the land while the price was good. There was just one problem, she said, no one was willing to buy the land at PhP 3,500 per square meter.

I had to tell her the sad news. The fact that no one was willing to buy the land only proves that its price is not really PhP 3,500 per square meter. More likely, the actual price would be around PHP 2,500 per square meter or PhP 500,000. At this price, her gain would only be PhP 100,000 over five years. This is just like earning interest at 4.6% per year. She could just as well have invested her original PhP 400,000 in government notes and earned more than 8% per year for the same period without any risk. As it was, she still ran the risk of not being able to sell the property.

I advised her to consult with reputable real estate brokers who were knowledgeable in the area where the property was located. I suggested that she engage them professionally to sell the property at the best possible price. That way she would have cash on hand and have the opportunity to let her money grow right away. Keeping that property made her "asset rich" but "cash poor".

Sapagkat hindi siya komunsulta bago namili, ngayon ay mayroon nga siyang lupa na hindi naman kumikita at hindi niya kailangan. Mas mabuti sana kung mayroon siyang cash. Ito ay maaaring kumita ng interes na walang peligro kung siya ay komunsulta sa talagang mapagkakatiwalaang propesyonal.

Seek professional and expert advice

Another common mistake that I have observed is our hesitance to go beyond our circle of friends and relatives when asking for financial advice. Often, we just blindly follow what our close relatives or friends have to say. We do not see the importance of seeking the advice of those who have the experience or expertise to give us sound financial advice.

Katulad nga ni Mr. F at Mrs. G, naniniwala sila sa kaibigan nilang matalik. Mabuti sana kung ang kaibigan nilang matalik ay tunay na propesyonal na marunong.

There are other money mistakes that may not be as glaring but are definitely just as costly. Some of these mistakes include our bad spending habits that are basically driven by our desire for immediate gratification. From active and primary income, we buy things we don't need, and worse, things we cannot really afford, by using our credit cards because we want to enjoy the benefits immediately.

These will be further discussed in the coming chapters.

In this chapter, I have given you a few examples of money mistakes that people make. Maybe you have committed one or two (or even more) of the mistakes I have mentioned here. You need not worry. No matter how many money mistakes you have committed in the past there is still hope. You can still attain financial freedom, but you have to start your journey now.

Huwag mabahala sa mga nakaraang pagkakamali.
Mag-umpisa ulit ngayon! Kaya mo ito!

You can do it. *Kaya mo 'to!*

- Everyone makes money mistakes but one must learn from those mistakes.

  Lahat ay nagkakamali sa paghawak ng pera ngunit kailangan tayong matuto sa ating mga pagkakamali.

- Always make sure that you understand exactly how earnings will be produced by the business you are investing in. It is not prudent for you to put out money just because a trusted friend says so.

  Laging intindihin ang proseso ng inaalok na negosyo na makapagbibigay ng kita sa puhunan mo. Huwag basta-bastang magpadala sa mga payo ng mga kaibigan o kamag-anak lalo na kung sila ay walang pagsasanay sa larangan ng "investments".

- You need to have a personal financial plan.

  Ang bawat isa sa atin ay kailangang may pansariling planong pinansyal.

- You must seek professional and expert advice when necessary.

  Kung kinakailangan, humanap ng propesyonal at dalubhasang tagapayo.

CHAPTER 4

What is Financial Independence

Plan, save and build wealth using what you have right now.

MOST OF US are pre-occupied with earning money. We pour time, talent, effort and resources into making money. Many employees take on extra jobs or put up small businesses to augment their salaries.

Very often, unfortunately, this drive to earn money is not founded on a meaningful personal financial plan. Financial objectives are not defined. We over-emphasize the importance of having more earnings without balancing this out with some initiative and plan to save. Few among us deliberately save a portion of our current earnings. It is as if our capacity to earn will not diminish over time. We refuse to see that as we grow older, and our bodies become weaker, our capacity to actively earn will greatly decrease.

This is the main reason very few of us become financially independent by the time we retire from our jobs. What happens most of the time, especially in our culture, is that when a parent is no longer able to work, it is the children, or other relatives, who take over the task of providing for the parent's financial needs. But this does not have to be the case all the time.

Kontra sa paniniwala ng nakararami, ang paglaya sa kakapusan ay abot-kaya ng lahat.

Contrary to common belief, financial independence is within everyone's reach. And that includes the average Filipino worker, or anyone who is capable of earning active income right now. This is true even if most of us have been conditioned to believe that we will never really have enough as we need to provide for our children's needs, the needs of their children, and, for some, even for the needs of their grandchildren.

Isang isyu sa ating kultura ay yung sobrang pag-ako ng mga magulang sa mga pangangailangang pinansyal ng kanilang anak at pati na ng kanilang mga apo. Dahil dito akala ng nakararami ay lagi silang kulang sa pera.

If you are currently employed or if you own a small business, you certainly have the potential to become financially independent in the future. The key lies in being able to plan, save, and build wealth using what you have now.

What is wealth and when is a person wealthy?

The concept of wealth is usually equated to having lots and lots of money. In reality, having money, even lots of money, is no assurance that one is automatically wealthy and can therefore afford to stop working for money. Wealth and money means nothing unless it is matched with time and expenses.

Are you wealthy if you had PhP 1 Million in your pocket? What about PhP 2 Million, PhP 10 Million or PhP 100 Million? The answer lies in your expense profile. If your living expenses are very high because of your lifestyle, or perhaps because you have so much debt, then maybe even if you had PhP 100 Million, you would still be financially short.

Wealth is really a condition where your present financial resources can support your lifestyle over a long period of time even if you do not work to generate income.

Ang tamang tanong ay: "Kung ikaw ngayon ay titigil ng magtrabaho gaano katagal kang mabubuhay ng iyong mga naimpok, napamuhunan, o ng iyong mga ari-arian?

So if you had cash and other financial assets that can support your lifestyle for, say, ten years, would you consider yourself wealthy?

Wealth or **kayamanan** has to be also based on how much time you have left in this world. If you are in retirement and have ten years to go, then you are wealthy enough if you had financial assets good to support your lifestyle for ten years. But if you only have resources good for five years, then you are not wealthy enough. In this case, you still have to grow your financial assets or lower your lifestyle to match your financial capability.

Ang pagpapasya kung ikaw ay mayroon nang sapat na kasaganaang pinansyal (kayamanan) ay naiiba sa bawat isang tao. Maaaring milyun-milyon ang iyong mga kita at mga ari-ariang pinansyal, ngunit ikaw ay di pa rin maluwag kung ikaw ay baon sa utang at ang antas ng iyong pamumuhay ay napakataas na halos isang kahig isang tuka lang din ang pamumuhay mo.

Hindi kailangang napakadami ang iyong salapi upang magkaroon ng tunay na kayamanan. Ang puno't dulo nito ay kung ang iyong mga napamuhunanan ay kayang tustusan ang iyong pamumuhay sa nalalabi mo pang panahon sa mundong ito.

Wealth-generation starts with a financial resource. For most of us, our base financial resource is our personal income. It is therefore very important that we have a clear understanding of the character and nature of income.

Kaya natin lumikha ng isang kasaganaang pinansyal sa pamamagitan ng pagpapalago ng ating kita o personal income. Kailangan lang na magkaroon tayo ng wastong pag-intindi ng iba't ibang uri ng kita.

38

Let me then discuss the two different kinds of income. One is Active Income, and the other is Passive Income.

Active Income

This is income that comes directly as a result of your own hard work, your skill, talent and time is active income.

Ang "Active Income" ay kita na galing sa ating aktibong pagtatrabaho, paggamit ng ating talento at paglagak ng ating panahon.

Once you stop working you stop earning active income.

There are two basic types of active income, namely, Primary and Additional:

Primary Income - Your main source of income: This would be your regular source of earning such as salaries, allowances, commissions, and contractual and/or professional fees

Additional Income - Income from your "sidelines" This could be irregular income such as overtime pay, income from "buy & sell" part-time, non-regular earnings from sources outside your primary income, such as gain from sale of assets and the like.

Active Income is income that you have to work for. It is the engine that starts your journey toward financial independence.

One rule that needs to be strictly followed is that active income should only be used:

:💡: to fund your living expenses and

:💡: to fund your savings and investments to generate future income for you.

Active income is reserved precisely to fuel your way toward wealth and financial freedom.

Spend active income only for your needs. NEVER for your wants.

Ang active income ay ginagamit lang para sa tunay na pangangailangan upang mabuhay at sa pagpapalago sa iyong naiimpok. Ito ay hindi dapat gastusin para sa luho.

Passive Income

This is income that is generated by your earning assets and investments is passive income. This is income that does not depend on your active participation in terms of time, skill or talent.

Ang "Passive Income" ay kita na galing sa pamumuhunan ng salapi o ari-arian kahit wala kang partisipasyon sa pagsasagawa nito.

Passive Income is income you earn even when you do not work.

Passive income is investment income. It is income that you earn from your assets or investments or both.

Because passive income is earned from your savings and investments, it has two main purposes:

- To further increase your investments that will fund your future needs when you have to stop working or when you decide to stop earning active income.

  Passive income represents your true wealth. It is not "gambling" money. Just because you do not use it for your current expenses, doesn't mean that you can do with it as you please. Passive income is your **REAL FINANCIAL GOAL**. You must always be aware of the growth or movement of your passive income. It will determine your financial success or failure.

- To fund your periodic wants. This should be your only source from which you may draw to use for the extra things you want from time to time (e.g. occasional parties, vacation, better car, nicer watch, fashionable clothes, etc.)

The appreciation of active and passive income is where most of us fail. We rationalize and spend our active income for wants much more than our needs. The behavior of PJ in our

Chapter One is a clear example. Because he had the money from his active income, he bought a Pajero. PJ used active income to pay for his wants.

He really needed a car. But did he need to buy a Pajero using his active income?

My view is that he should have:

 bought a cheaper but useful and reliable car first.

 saved the difference in cost and invested it to earn interest.

given himself some more time and let his investment accumulate earnings.

 set fixed financial goals and once achieved, he could use this passive income to upgrade his car to a Pajero.

Financial Independence

Marami sa atin ay naniniwala na tanging malaking halagang salapi at ari-arian lang ang makapagdudulot sa atin ng tunay na Kalayaan sa Kakapusan (KsK). Walang katotohanan ito!

Most of us believe the myth that financial independence means having so much money and assets. As I said earlier, we focus purely on earnings and the so-called build-up of wealth.

...lth just having cash to ... If you believe this, then ... without having very ... odest, then all you need ... you would be financially ... Santos described in the ... lity.

... g the means to maintain ... out having to actively ... where your personal ... assive income sufficient ... the level and type of ...

Pa... ... to KsK or Financial In... ... come, you will never a...

... ang susi ... an sa iyong ... kapusan.

Fo... ly salary allows you to ha... If you are to become fin... accumulate earning ass... rate earnings that will all... of lifestyle by the time you...

Sta... ly independent when you... ger have to work to ...

provide for your basic needs. This means that your passive income, or the money you earn through your assets and investments, are enough to provide for your daily needs such as food, shelter, clothing, education of your children, medical expenses, and even some luxuries.

Ang halimbawa ni Ms. Marilou Santos

Let me cite as an example Marilou Santos (not her real name), a 35-year-old Filipina who has been working in Hong Kong for the past three years. Her monthly net salary is HK$ 4,200 or PhP 30,000 and she estimates her monthly expenses to be PhP 20,000. If she wants to maintain that same amount of monthly income and if the prevailing interest rate is 12%, she needs to save and accumulate investments and/or earning assets of at least PhP 2 million. PhP 2 million at 12% per year would generate annual revenue of PhP 240,000 a year, or PhP 20,000 a month.

Alternatively, if her investments will only earn 10% instead of 12% annually, Marilou will then need to save and accumulate PhP 2.4 million of earning assets instead of PhP 2 million mentioned above, in order to meet her monthly expenses of PhP 20,000.

This simplified example does not take into account inflation, which would reduce purchasing power and personal income taxes that may be due from her active earnings. If she takes inflation and taxes into account, she will need to have a higher income and therefore more earning assets and investments, or she can adjust her lifestyle. For now, we will simply assume that personal taxes will be minimal as her offshore income is probably and practically tax-free.

Ginawa ko lang simple ang halimbawang ito upang maumpisahan ang pag-iisip natin. Katulad ng sinabi ko, kailangan nating magtanong sa marurunong na propesyonal upang mabigyan tayo ng tamang payo.

Financial independence can be achieved at any age. You just need to plan for it.

Let me note that you do not have to wait to be 65 years old before you can achieve financial independence.

Maaari kang magplano ng iyong pinansyal na kinabukasan na patungo sa retirement sa kahit na anong edad mong nais.

I am 59 years old right now. Because I want to be actively engaged in my profession, I am still earning active income. But if tomorrow I suddenly decide to stop working, I know that the investments and earning assets I have will provide me with passive income that will be more than enough to maintain the kind of lifestyle that I have chosen.

I must admit though, that it was only in the past decade that I started to actively practice the personal finance principles that I am sharing with you now. I know that if I had started practicing the personal finance habits that this book aims to teach, I would have achieved financial independence at a much earlier age. And today, I would have a lot more earning assets and investments. These investments would be providing many more benefits than what I am currently enjoying. I would then have more financial resources to spend for myself and/or to share with my family and my community.

Financial Independence empowers you to enhance the lives of your chosen community.

Achieving financial independence early on in your life is probably one of the greatest gifts you can give to your family and your chosen community. Without doubt, the ability to share your bounty with others can be the greatest source of satisfaction and the most fulfilling human experience. Being financially independent affords you more opportunities to enhance the lives of others and, through them, even other communities. Isn't that what money is for? A tool to improve everyone's well being?

Saving and accumulating sufficient investments and earning assets take time. This is one fundamental truth that most of us seem to take for granted. We always assume that there will always be enough time to work on our financial requirements for retirement. Worse, the mentality of those who retire is that their pension benefits would be enough to take care of their needs.

Paulit-ulit kong sinasabi sapagkat ito ay mahalaga. Matagal ang mag-impok ng sapat na halaga na kikita ng sapat na passive income. Kailangang umpisahan mo na ang paglalakbay patungo sa kalayaan sa kakapusan ngayon! Nauubos ang iyong panahon at ang mga oportunidad upang palaguin ang iyong pera. Kung ang iyong mga anak at kamag-anak ay umaasa sa pera mo ngayon, mas mabuti kung hindi ka naman aasa sa pera nila sa iyong pagtanda.

You can do it. *Kaya mo 'to!*

- Active income comes directly from your own hard work.

  Ang "Active Income" ay galing sa sarili mong sikap.

- Passive income comes from earnings of your assets and investments.

  Ang "Passive Income" ay galing sa interes o tubo ng iyong ari-arian at puhunan.

- Being wealthy means you have passive income that can support your chosen lifestyle until the day you die.

  Ikaw ay mayaman kung ang "Passive Income" mo ay sapat na buhayin ka sa antas na pamumuhay na ayon sa iyong kagustuhan hanggang ikaw ay pumanaw.

CHAPTER 5

Your Obstacles To Financial Freedom

Recognize and accept obstacles - then take action against them.

THE STRUGGLE FOR financial independence is private and individual: yours alone. You alone can chart the course of your financial future. If you desire it, you can achieve financial success. However, it is easier said than done! There are several fundamental obstacles to achieving financial independence. You need to recognize these and more importantly, you have to accept them and then take action.

These are:

● **_Procrastination_** *(Pagpapabukas)* - Filipinos are known procrastinators. We have this *"mañana"* habit of putting off for tomorrow what we can accomplish today. Do not procrastinate; it will cost you dearly. If you delay saving PhP 3,000 earning 10% per year for just ONE YEAR, you will lose more than PhP 137,000 forty years from now, an amount equivalent to the down payment for an FX. Can you really afford not to have this amount? And for what? For the cost of doing away with one soft drink can per day?

Delaying savings decisions may also mean passing up opportunities. Certain investment instruments offering high interest rates (yields) may no longer be available by the time you decide to save. An example would be certain government bonds, which used to be offering up to 14% or 15% are now just yielding 10%. Everyday, we see examples of missed opportunities about people who failed to take advantage of cheaper homes, cheaper loans and the like, because they delayed making their decision. In most cases, perhaps by force of habit, they put off for tomorrow what they could decide today. Not only do missed opportunities cost you money, they actually cause you to lose real wealth.

● **_Inflation_** - The economic condition of sustained price increases. Money is an asset that continuously loses value. When prices of . commodities go up, the value of money decreases. In order to maintain or improve your personal wealth, you must find a way to beat inflation.

I remember the days when as I young boy, the cost of a bottle of soft drink was ten centavos. Today, that bottle of soft drink sells for an average price of nine pesos. This increase in price translates to approximately 9.8% increase per year. This would not be a problem for me if my income level also increased at 9.8% per year. If however, my income has not increased at the same or higher rate than this, then I will no longer be able to afford to buy soft drinks. Fortunately, since I don't drink soft drinks regularly, this particular inflation of soft drink prices does not affect or bother me at all.

But what about the inflation rate, which applies to rice or sugar or chicken, or other goods that people consume?

Today, our annual inflation rate is estimated at about 4%. This means that the average prices of certain key commodities, which the majority of our people consume on a regular basis, are increasing every year by 4%. Because of this, we must make sure that our incomes and our savings and investments grow by at least 4% or better. Otherwise, we will be reducing our purchasing power. For the same amount of money as last year, we will not be able to buy the same amount of goods this year.

Inflation is a condition that is sure to stay with us. It has been so with all countries and with all economies all over the world. This is as certain as night follows day.

Inflation is much like a creeping disease. It is like a fever that starts very lightly and slowly increases until you realize too late that you have become seriously ill.

Ang epekto ng implasyon ay mailalarawan sa tinatawag na "boiling frog syndrome". Kung ang palaka ay ilalagay sa tubig na kumukulo, ito ay mabilis na tatalong palabas. Pero kung ito ay ilalagay sa kalderong may tubig na unti-unting pinakukuluan, di mapapansin agad ito at maaari pa siyang masarapan. Ngunit sa daloy ng oras, unti-unti siyang maluluto hanggang siya ay mamatay.

It is, therefore, not enough to just save. Where you put your savings will determine whether your earnings rate will beat inflation. This is very important because these financial instruments will be the source of the growth of your savings. As a rule, you should target an earnings rate, that is 4% higher than inflation.

Ang implasyon ay walang epekto sa ating kakayanang pinansyal kung ang ating kinikita ay nadadagdagan ng higit pa sa antas ng implasyon. Ganoon din kung ang ating mga naimpok o napamuhunan ay kumikita taun-taon nang higit pa sa taas ng mga presyo ng mga pangkaraniwang bilihin. Kaya nga kung gusto nating masiguro ang ating kalayaan sa kakapusan, ang dapat nating tiyakin ay kumita ng mga apat na porsyentong (4%) karagdagan sa antas ng implasyon.

● **Unreasonable Demands of Family and Friends** - Oftentimes, family and friends expect support to the point of unreasonableness. There are many stories about brothers and sisters who give up their own happiness just to ensure that their younger brothers and sisters are properly educated.

It is so familiar a picture in barangays all over the country where the family members of the OFW spend their time doing nothing while waiting for the remittance of the OFW. Come remittance day, the barangay goes into fiesta mode. The money that was sent for education or for investment in a business is diverted to unnecessary recreation, drinking session, gambling and good time. The poor OFW discovers all these only after he/she comes home.

When the OFW returns home, everyone expects a pasalubong so that the hard earned money quickly disappears.

Ways to combat:

- Educate your family and friends as you are educating yourself on financial matters. Tell them about this book and if possible, let them read and learn from it.

- Arrange to send money for education directly to the school or buy a Pre-need education plan from a reputable Pre-need company.

- Buy a pension plan from a reputable Pre-need company to ensure that you have some retirement money.

- Prepare your financial plan and stick to it.

Anyayahan ang iyong pamilya sa isang tapat na talakayan ng kahalagahan ng pansariling planong pinansyal. Tulungan mo silang unawain ang iyong kalagayan at ang iyong layunin sa pagtatrabaho sa ibang bansa. Ipabasa sa kanila ang aklat na ito upang ang buong kamag-anakan mo ay magkaroon ng tamang pag-intindi ng tamang planong pinansyal.

● **Yourself** - Negative values can hinder us from achieving financial independence as well as from succeeding in other areas of our life. Our fear of failure, laziness, negativism, bad spending habits, lack of emotional and financial intelligence can keep us from succeeding in life. Fortunately, all it takes is determination, decisiveness and desire to overcome these and they are all within your power. Don't be a loser. Be guided by winners. As they say: Losers criticize. Winners analyze.

Negative Values to overcome:

● **Fear of failure** - Most people are so afraid to make mistakes that they end up not doing anything. They only see why they are bound to fail and not how they can succeed. You should be guided by the fact that failure is part and parcel of success. You cannot succeed unless you once failed. There is nothing to fear about failure. What is important is what you learn from that painful experience. Pain is a very powerful tool to move you into action. It is a great motive. And in any endeavor, motivation is a fundamental requirement for success.

Walang nagtatagumpay na hindi dumaan sa pagkabigo.

Looking at the other side of failure shows you its many other advantages. To fail:

- means that you have put some effort and that you have actually attempted to achieve something you want. This is a very good indication that you have what it takes to succeed.

- gives you the opportunity to learn a better way of doing things - another very positive addition to your bank of knowledge!

- teaches you something to add to your experience. This is very helpful as you move on to try to achieve new objectives in your future.

Failure is an event. It is not a person.

Ang pagkabigo ay isang pangyayari. Hindi ikaw ito.
Huwag kang masiraan ng loob. Tingnan mo
ang magandang aral na iyong natutunan dahil dito
at lalong uunlad ang iyong kakayahan.
Gawin mong maestro ang pagkabigo.
Huwag mo siyang hayaang maging taga-libing mo.

● **Laziness** - Many of us have developed the habit of too much dependence on others. This has led to indolence and sheer laziness. We seem to take it for granted that when we face a crisis, someone, something, somewhere will appear to help us out. This war for financial independence is a personal war. It has to be fought individually. We cannot let somebody else fight it for us. We can only win it if we prepare ourselves for it and then take action on our own.

- **Poor spending habits** - This is one of the most serious concerns that you have to learn to understand and control. If you look around you, you will find that most of your expenses are really optional, meaning, they are not necessary. One of the quickest ways to control this is to list down all your actual expenses on a daily basis and sum them up at the end of each month. Do this for three months and you will have a very good idea where your money goes.

Most likely, you will find out that over half of your expenses can be considered as unnecessary or perhaps at least as postponable. Why is this so? I believe there are two major reasons that account for this behavior:

- **Impulse buying** - People, especially those who do "malling" for leisure, almost always end up buying more than what they intended to. The sales and promotions for products and services aggressively marketed in the malls sway them. The regular "midnight sale" at the malls never fail to attract consumers both new and old. They seem to be drawn to the idea that they are saving money by buying discounted products even though they have no real use for them yet. It would not be surprising to find out that some of these items bought on sale are never used and just end up inside closets, to be given out as gifts or to charity, later on.

- **Spending because of trends** *(Uso kasi)* - So many of our young employees, agents and professionals spend their hard-earned salaries and commissions on truly unnecessary items. They like to continuously upgrade their cell phones every time new models are introduced.

Personal beauty accessories, hair products and services and fashion jewelry are also very high in the priority of spending. Among women professionals, perhaps the highest spending is on fashion items, cosmetic products and cosmetic medical services, like liposuction, face and nose lifts and so many others.

Masyadong matindi ang impluwensya ng uso sa paggastos, halimbawa: cell phones, usong damit at usong cosmetics. Sa tutuusin, hindi talaga kailangan agad-agad bumili nito. Ngunit, marami pa rin ang hindi makahintay at dali-daling bumibili kapag nagkaroon lang ng kahit kaunting pera.

Your spending habit is the final determinant of your financial success. What really counts is not so much what you earn but what you get to keep. In-between lies your spending behavior. You must learn to be continuously vigilant of your progress towards financial independence. This is a task that must be assessed daily. Every time you spend or disburse money, ask yourself the question - "Will this bring me closer to my financial goal?" Remember, you, and only you, have the power to achieve your goal. Use it!

"We cannot control the wind. But we can adjust our sails."

Anonymous

Lack of financial literacy

Very often, people make spending decisions based on an erroneous understanding of money and assets. They spend on what they believe are assets when in fact they are really liabilities. When this happens, they lose on two counts, namely:

- They incur a loss because they will not recover the same amount of money if and when they sell those items that they believe are assets.

- They further incur a loss of opportunity. Money that is spent for a specific purpose is no longer available to be used for other purposes. That is why if you lose PhP 1,000 because of a bad transaction, you actually lose the opportunity of growing this PhP 1,000 into PhP 2,594 in ten years if it had been invested in a security that gives ten percent interest per year.

This is why it is so important that you realize that every time you spend, you must have an idea of how much you are giving up by not investing that amount. This is particularly true if what you spend for is not really all that necessary.

Ang pisong nagastos na sa isang bagay ay pisong hindi na pwedeng ilagak sa pamumuhunan na maaaring magbigay ng kita upang mapalago ang inyong kayamanang pinansyal. Kaya napakahalaga na intindihin muna kung ang isang gastusin ay talagang kailangan. Kung opsyonal din lang naman, huwag na muna gastusin at ilagak na lang ito para sa inyong kinabukasang pinansyal.

Most of us never go beyond our own borders of education and experience. Those who do not have extensive formal education feel that they are permanently disadvantaged because they have not studied finance and accounting and other related courses. They end up asking the wrong people for financial advice and some have, in fact, suffered heavily because of bad advice.

This mindset should be reversed. Financial literacy is all about common sense. It is knowing what real wealth means and what money is for, the difference between assets and liabilities, the value of money against inflation (time value of money) and the means available to build up personal financial worth over time. People must realize that this does not require formal college degrees. They can be financially literate through self-study and attending basic personal finance seminars. This book, I hope, will in many ways, help build your literacy in financial matters.

You can do it. *Kaya mo 'to!*

- Recognize and accept your personal obstacle to financial freedom.

  Kinakailangan mong maintindihan at makilala ang iyong sarili. Ano ang mga sagabal o hadlang sa iyong kalayaan sa kakapusan?

- Do not delay. Take appropriate action right away.

  Huwag ipagliban. Gumawa agad ng mga hakbang patungo sa pag-alam ng mga tamang pamamahala ng salapi.

- Be a winner. Be positive in all that you do. Do not be afraid to fail. Failure is an integral part of success.

  Walang nagtatagumpay na hindi dumaan sa pagkabigo.

CHAPTER 6

Your Allies
To Financial Freedom

| TIME | COMPOUND INTEREST | LEVERAGE |

*Time, compound interest and leverage
are your strong allies.*

DON'T LOSE HEART. Just as you have the above "enemies" that prevent you from winning this war for financial independence, you have strong "allies" by your side. They are there, just waiting for your call.

Time

Your first ally is "Father Time". Time, the great equalizer, is on your side. All of us, rich or poor, have the same amount of time. Twenty-four hours per day, seven days a week, twelve months a year. Time is a resource. It is particularly a great ally in planning for your financial independence. The key is timing, to know when to choose to invest or to divest.

Time is the most taken-for-granted resource. This is very clearly demonstrated by what is negatively attributed to Filipinos as "Filipino time". We are always looked upon as perennial latecomers that it is no longer funny. We don't seem to understand that every time we are late for an appointment and cause other parties to wait, we are actually stealing from them their own time resource! If you make me wait for an hour, you have actually stolen one hour from me, one hour that I could have used to earn income but which I have now completely lost. That "one-hour" is gone forever and you made me lose it!

Ang "Filipino time," na ang kahulugan ay parating huli sa oras na tipan ay sikapin nating burahi't palitan, pagkat ito'y mantsa sa ating pangalan.

Francisco "Soc" Rodrigo

62

I recall an economic study that concluded that punctuality was one of the major success factors of Japan. People there, especially businessmen, are seldom late for their appointments. Consequently, they almost always, perhaps by force of habit, make sure they always meet their business deadlines. Time may seem to be an insignificant factor, but the reality is time is money.

Kapag ang "ngayon" mo ay maging "kahapon"
Nang wala kang kahit kaunti mang pabaon,
Di baga't nasayang ang panahong yaon?

Francisco "Soc" Rodrigo

Compound Interest

Your second ally is Compound Interest. According to Dr. Albert Einstein, "Compound interest is man's greatest invention". Great wealth can be created if we allow the power of compound interest and time to work for us. We see this power every day around us. Investments allowed to compound can help you beat inflation.

We will discuss this further in Chapter 16.

Leverage

Finally, another very powerful ally is within our reach. It is the power of leverage. This power is sometimes referred to as Good Debt. Debt used for productive investments increases your financial returns even with very little capital. Leverage allows you to grow your investments five or even 10 times faster than if you were to do it alone. Leverage refers to people as well as to money. Pooling of resources multiplies your gains while minimizing your risks. Legitimate multi-level marketing and business systems are also other forms of leverage. They allow you to earn through your "down lines" even without being active in selling.

Leverage or pingga ay ang pamamaraan ng paggamit ng mga bagay o samahan ng mga tao na nakakapagbigay ng gaan sa mga ginagawa o pagpapalago ng kita. Yung mga nakapagpalaki ng kanilang mga negosyo sa pamamagitan ng utang ay isang halimbawa sa paggamit ng pingga or leverage. Bayanihan at paluwagan ay mga iba pang halimbawa nito.

These allies will ensure your success. They are on stand-by. All you need to do is to call on them.

In the succeeding chapters, I will discuss the different steps you need to achieve financial independence.

The key to financial independence lies in being able to plan, save, and build wealth using what you have now.

You can do it. *Kaya mo 'to!*

You have allies to help you achieve financial freedom.
These are **Time, Compound interest and Leverage**.
Understand these allies as explained in the following
chapters.

*Mayroon kang kakampi sa pagtamo ng kalayaan sa
kakapusan. Ito ay Panahon, "Compound Interest"
at "Leverage" o ang paggamit ng pingga o panikwas.
Intindihing maigi ang mga kakamping ito na
tinatalakay sa susunod na yugto.*

CHAPTER 7

Know Where You Are

Knowing where you are tells you how far you are going and how to get there.

AFTER READING the previous chapters, you must now be excited to start your journey to financial freedom. There is still hope for you even after all the mistakes you have committed in the past. So now you're thinking: "In five years I want to have a nice house and a brand new car and a monthly passive income of at least PhP 100,000." Sounds good. You really think you can make it. It's possible!

But wait, before you even start thinking of your destination, you must first determine where you are right now. You cannot plan for your journey unless you first figure out where you are now financially. By knowing where you are, you will be able to determine how far you are from your destination, the kind of journey you have to take, and the kind of vehicle that you need to use.

Kung ikaw ay bago sa isang mall at naghahanap ka ng isang partikular na shop, hindi ba pupuntahan mo ang building directory? At ano ang unang makikita mo doon? Kadalasan, ang makikita mo ay isang karatula na naglalahad ng mga direksyon tungkol sa lokasyon ng bawat shop. At ang pinakaunang pahayag sa iyo ay "You are here". Ang senyas na ito ay nagbibigay ng patunay na upang makarating ka sa nais mong puntahan, dapat alam mo kung saan ka magsisimula. Kung alam mo ang iyong kasalukuyang kinalalagyan, madali mong mabibigyang halaga ang layo o lapit ng lugar na nais mong puntahan. Ganyan din ang kailangang gawin hinggil sa pag-unawa ng mga hakbang patungo sa Kalayaan sa Kakapusan.

Knowing where you are financially means knowing:

- what assets and other resources you have

- how much debt and other obligations you have

- what you are worth financially today (your net worth)

- how much income you are generating

- how much you are spending

Knowing these would enable you to analyze if you have been spending your money wisely, how much money you need to save to achieve your desired net worth, and what your priorities should be.

Hindi ito mahirap. Kung hindi ka sanay, aakalain mo na mahirap. Ngunit kung pag-uukulan mo lang ng kaunting panahon, kaya mo ito!

Preparation of your Personal Financial Statements

You would need to prepare two very important financial statements to find out where you are exactly. (Relax; you do not have to be an accountant to prepare these financial statements.) The first financial statement you have to make is your Personal Statement of Assets *(Ari-Arian)* and Liabilities *(Utang)* (SAL). Your SAL will show your personal net worth. The second is your Personal Income-Expense *(Kita-Gastos)* Statement (PIES). Your PIES gives you the details of all your sources of income and the listing of all types of expenses you incur. More likely, this listing will show you what expenses are necessary and what are unnecessary.

In making your SAL, what you need to do is to basically list down all the money and properties you own (Assets *o Ari-arian*) and the money that you owe other people or institutions (Liabilities *o Utang*).

In your Assets column, you should include the following:

- Cash
  This includes your savings deposits, current deposits, time deposits and cash on hand.

- Properties that you own
  House, land, car, or jewelry, whether they have been fully paid or not. If possible, you should list down the estimated current market or re-sale value of your property. (For example, to get an estimated re-sale value of your car, divide the cost price by five years to get the yearly depreciation then multiply the yearly depreciation by the number of years you have used the car and subtract it from the cost of the car).

- Receivables
  Money that others owe you. These are amounts you may have lent to a relative or friend, which are not yet paid; pending collections from clients for services you have rendered; or goods or property you have sold but are not yet paid for.

- Investments
  Includes all investments in businesses of any kind, government securities (such as Treasury bills or Treasury bonds, shares of stock and other types of investments).

- Insurance and pension and academic plans
  The cash surrender value of all your insurance policies.

In your Liabilities column include:

- Loans you owe your relatives and friends.

- Housing loan.

- Car loan

- Credit card debt.

- All payables and other loans.

After getting the sum total of both the Assets and Liabilities columns, subtract your Total Liabilities from your Total Assets to get your Net Worth.

Total Assets - Total Liabilities = Net Worth

This is how the SAL of Marilou Santos (refer to Chapter 4) looks like:

STATEMENT OF ASSETS & LIABILITIES
MARILOU SANTOS in PhP
AS OF DEC 31, 2003

ASSETS

Personal na Pag Aari (Assets)		650,000
House & Lot	500,000	
Furnitures	50,000	
Appliances	60,000	
Alahas	10,000	
Clothes & others	30,000	
Savings & Investments		80,000
Cash	5,000	
Savings Deposits	25,000	
Government Securities	50,000	
Retirement Savings		500,000
Pension	500,000	
TOTAL ASSETS		1,230,000

Note: The entry of the pension maturity value is not in accordance with accounting standards. However, as a personal tool, it is very effective to book your pension or savings plan at maturity value. The premiums still payable must be entered in the liability column in order to remind yourself of the gain in net worth you can expect if you religiously pay your premium payments.

LIABILITIES

Personal Debts (Payables)		626,340
Bahay (includes interest)	526,500	
Appliances (credit card)	39,840	
Auto	–	
Other Credit Card Debts	–	
Utang para makaalis ng bansa	60,000	
Investment Debt		203,040
Business Loan	–	
Investment Loan	–	
Pension - PreNeed	203,040	
Insurance Loan	–	
Others:	–	
TOTAL LIABILITIES		829,380
PERSONAL NETWORTH		400,620
TOTAL LIABILITIES & NETWORTH		1,230,000

NOTES: List of Assets and Liabilities
1. House purchase: PhP500,000; down payment of Php 100,000; Php 400,000 loan at PhP3,375/mo for 15 yrs at 6% per year; Status: 2 yrs paid; now on third yr; PhP526,000 payable over next 13 years.
2. Php 100,000 worth of appliances; Php 50,000 by credit card at

PhP1,660/mo for 2 more years; total payable still at Php 39,480.
3. *Loan for recruitment ; Php 60,000 still payable at Php 2,000/mo.*
4. *Php 500,000 pension plan at 10/20 terms; Monthly premium is Php 1,880; 9 more years to pay; balance is Php 203,040.*

After drawing up your SAL, you need to prepare a monthly PIES so you can clearly see where all your income is coming from. It will also show how you are spending that income.

Your PIES should provide the following details:

Salary
Interest Income from Savings and Time Deposits
Income from Investments in Government Securities and Stocks
Income from other assets
Less: Expenses
    Food
    Rent
    Monthly amortization for housing, car and other loans
    Utilities
    Insurance premiums
    Allowance of Children
    Tuition Fee
    Other Expenses
Net Income
Less: Personal Income Tax
Net Income After Tax

(Gross Income - Expenses -Taxes= Net Income After Tax)

For your reference, this is how the PIES of Marilou Santos looks like:

PERSONAL STATEMENT OF INCOME & EXPENSE NI MARILOU SANTOS in PhP

Salary: HK$4,200+ eqyal to PhP 30,000 per month

ACTIVE:	
Primary: Sahod	PHP 30,000
Additional; (Sidelines)	5,600
PASSIVE: SECONDARY	
Interest income	300
Other Income (Lupa)	0
GROSS INCOME	35,900
LESS: LIVING EXPENSES:	
Food (Pamalengke at Groceries)	9,000
Renta sa bahay	0
Gastos sa bahay (ex. Gasul, etc)	1,000
Pamasahe	1,500
Cellphone	1,500
Kuryente	1,500
Tubig	500
Allowance-"Baon ng mga bata"	2,000
Eskwelahan	1,000

TOTAL: LIVING EXPENSES	18,000

R & R (OPTIONAL EXPENSES)

-movies/"pasyal"	2,000	
-clothes/personal (etc)	2,000	
Babasahin	1,000	
Biglaan gastos (Gifts, etc)	1,000	
TOTAL: OPTIONAL EXPENSES		6,000

OTHER CASH PAYMENTS

House Amortization	3,375	
Credit cards	1,660	
Other personal debts	2,000	
Pension plans	1,880	
TOTAL: OTHER CASH PAYMENTS		8,915

TOTAL: MONTHLY EXPENSES	32,915
Net Income	2,985
INCOME TAX (Exempted)	0
Net Income After Tax	2,985

Inuulit ko na hindi ito ang ginagamit ng mga korporasyon sa kanilang accounting. Inaakma ko lamang ito sa ating personal na gamit upang makatulong sa ating pagsuri ng ating pinansyal na kalagayan.

Determine your Financial Life Phase

After computing your income and expenses you can then determine what life phase you are in financially:

- **Start-up Phase** - You are deemed to be on Start-up Phase when practically all your income is active income. This means that your only source of income is salary or commission or allowance or income from buy and sell or such other income generated by dedicating your own time and talent actively. This is the time when you do not have anything but active income to pay for all of your needs and expenses.

- **Build-up Phase** - You are on Build-up Phase when you have assets and investments generating passive income that accounts for about 20% of your total income, and that is sufficient to fund at least 20% of your needs and expenses.

- **Asset Allocation Phase** - You are on Asset Allocation Phase when you have assets and investments generating passive income that accounts for about 30% to 60% of your total income and is able to fund at least 50% of your personal needs and expenses.

- **Retirement Phase** -You are on Retirement Phase when you can afford to stop earning active income and rely only on your passive income to support your needs, expenses, and wants.

It is important to review your SAL on a yearly basis and your PIES on a monthly basis. This will allow you to keep your focus on the growth of your Net Worth every year. You will then be able to see how you are getting closer to or farther from to your financial goals. This would also allow you to make necessary adjustments year by year. Tracking your personal Net Worth every year is key to achieving your **KsK**.

Taun-taon ay ugaliin mong repasuhin ang iyong SAL upang makita mo ang pagsulong (o pag-atras) ng iyong Net Worth o Netong Halaga mo. Ang halagang ito ang tangi mong gabay sa iyong paglalakbay patungo sa Kalayaan sa Kakapusan.

You can do it. *Kaya mo 'to!*

- You cannot plan for your journey unless you know where you are financially today. By knowing where you are, you will be able to determine how far you are from your destination, the kind of journey you have to take, and the kind of vehicle that you need to use.

   Bago ang lahat, alamin mo ang iyong katayuang pinansyal. Ito ang iyong pasimula sa pagpapalago ng iyong kayamanan. Ito ang tanging batayan sa pagtuos ng iyong tunay na pag-aari sa pagplano ng iyong estratehiyang pinansyal.

- You will only know your financial standing when you complete your own Personal Statement of Income and Expenses (PIES) and Statement of Assets and Liabilities (SAL).

   Ipagpatuloy mo ang pagbabasa upang mas maintindihan mo kung papaano at kung ano ang gagawin mo sa iyong PIES at SAL.

CHAPTER 8

What is your unique genius?

Each of us has a unique genius that allows us to excel.

Hindi sapat na alam mo ang kalagayan mo sa larangang pampinansyal. Ang pagtagumpay dito ay may malaking kaugnayan sa mga aspetong personal. Dapat alamin mo saang bagay ka mahusay at saan ka mahina.

NOW THAT YOU know where you are financially, it is also critical to understand yourself better before you set out to determine your financial goals. Knowing who you are involves knowing what your strengths and weaknesses are, which would then enable you to craft your own winning formula for success.

The first step in knowing who you are is finding out your "genius". It has been widely acknowledged that there are seven multiple intelligences. Each of us is strong in some of these intelligences and weak in others. I have briefly explained each one of these seven intelligences below.

Assess your strengths and weaknesses

- **Verbal**

Has superior ability to use words, good at explaining things, likes writing and reading, able to absorb information and conceptualize details quickly. Can be a great teacher, a poet, a writer, a lawyer.

Magaling magsalita at magsulat,
Mahilig magbasa.

- **Visual/Spatial**

Has superior ability to clearly visualize things. Good in using charts & symbols to get his message across, can clearly picture how something will look like, can perceive dimensions. Can be an artist, an architect, a designer

Magaling gumuhit ng mga ideya.

From an article at www.ldpride.net by author E.Brood (Multiple intelligence was conceived by Dr. Howard Gardner)

80

• Physical or Kinetic

Has superior ability to use his body well. Learns best by touching and doing, likes working with his hands. Can be a great athlete, a dancer

Magaling ang koordinasyon ng lahat ng parte ng kanyang katawan.

• Musical

Has superior ability to understand and use music. Easily remembers tunes and lyrics, uses music as a frame of reference, has a natural sense of timing or rhythm, enjoys sounds of all types, is easily distracted by sounds, notices the cadence of things. Can be good musician, singer, composer

Magaling ang boses at tainga sa musika.

• Mathematical & Logical

Has superior ability to apply logic to systems and numbers. Likes putting things in order, arranges things logically, looks for patterns and relationships between things, good at analysis, calculation, planning. Can be good computer programmer, accountant, scientist, mathematician

Magaling sa numero at sa pagsusuri

• Introspective/Intrapersonal

Understands and analyzes his own thoughts and feelings, understands his own motives and reasons for doing things, likes to daydream about new ideas and explore his own feelings, reflective and thoughtful. Good as researcher, philosopher

Madaling makaunawa ng sarili at kung bakit ang mga pangyayari ay nagaganap.

• Interpersonal

Has superior ability to relate well to others. Can mediate arguments. Knows what to do to connect with someone else, sensitive to others, likes contact with people. A born leader. Will make good salesman, politician, businessman.

Magaling makisama sa kapwa at magaling makaimpluwensya ng iba.

Tanungin mo ang sarili mo kung saan ang galing o hilig mo. Suriin mong maigi kung ano ang talagang gusto mong gawin. Huwag magpadala sa isipan ng iba. Hanaping maigi ang nararapat at angkop na gawain para sa iyo.

Once you've figured out your strengths and weaknesses, you will be in a better position to avoid possible pitfalls or risks as you plan for the occupation or profession you will undertake in order to achieve financial targets. As you can see, each one of us possesses a genius unique to him or her. Everyone can excel in his or her own field of genius. Find your genius and use it to your advantage.

Knowing your genius will give you the edge to overcome whatever difficulties may come your way. It will help you choose what field of endeavor you will most likely succeed in. It will give you the self-confidence to try new things and not be afraid to fail.

Do you have a winning character?

The other side of the genius coin in life is character. Character is conviction. Character is commitment. Character, in the end, determines our fate. Genius without character is not enough. As there are no certainties in life except failure. No one achieves success without failing first. In fact, someone once said that the best way to accelerate success is to double your failure rate. The law of failure is one of the most powerful of all success laws.

Knowing that failure is a certainty, we must prepare ourselves to confront it when it happens. We must even learn how to recognize it before it gets worse. We must be clear about our financial goals. Above all we must not just be interested in achieving financial independence, we must stay committed to it.

"There is a difference between interest and commitment. When you are interested in doing something, you do it only when it is convenient. When you are committed to something, you accept no excuses, only results."

Kenneth Blanchard

My own experience, as well as those of Mr. PJ's, Mrs. AC's and Mr. F & Mrs. G's in the previous chapters, validates this reality. So many things out there are beyond our control. And yet, what may seem like problems, oftentimes, turn out to be opportunities.

"Life is ten percent what happens to us and ninety percent how we respond to it."

Anonymous

And yet, how should you respond when the unexpected happens? When all of a sudden, all the expectations you worked for do not happen? Do you quit? Do you run away from the problem? Or, do you analyze, prepare and try to overcome the problem?

Genius can only point to possible directions and solutions. Character will move you to action! In the final analysis, it is character that delivers your response to adversity.

Ang kabalikat ng henyo ay pagkatao. Ang paninindigan sa mga pananagutan ay ang katangian na siyang maghuhusga ng ating tagumpay o kabiguan. Ang henyo ay makapagtuturo lamang sa atin ng mga direksyon at mga alternatibong magagawa sa harap ng mga di inaasahang suliranin. Tanging pagkatao ang makapagpapagalaw sa atin.

Let us all remember that quitting is a permanent solution to a temporary problem. So whatever problems occur, there is a solution. Your genius can help you find it. But it is your character that will either make you use it or run away from it. So as early as now, develop that winning habit. Small successes every day will ensure your eventual victory over adversity.

Habang may buhay, hindi dapat tayo sumuko. Ang ating henyo at pagkatao ay magbibigay sa atin ng lakas upang magtagumpay! Ang sumusuko ay talo! Kaya natin ang lahat!

You can do it. *Kaya mo 'to!*

- Analyze your genius and choose the activities that match that genius. It is easier to achieve success when you match your particular talent with the demands of your work.

  Suriin ang iyong henyo at hanggang maaari, piliin ang trabaho o propesyon na angkop dito. Mas madaling magtagumpay kung maisagawa mo ito.

- Genius without character will result in failure. Character is commitment and commitment moves you to action.

  Ang kabalikat ng henyo ay pagkatao. Tanging pagkataong tapat ang makapagpapagalaw sa atin

Setting Your Financial Goal

*Put your goals in writing as you put
seeds into soil.*

HERE ARE SOME guide questions that will help you define your financial goals:

1   What level of lifestyle do you want? Do you want to just maintain your current lifestyle or do you want it to improve?   ***Tanggap mo na ba ang pamumuhay mo ngayon o gusto mo itong ibahin?***

2   How do you want your lifestyle to improve? For example, if you need Php 20,000 a month to maintain the lifestyle you have now, how much more do you need to enjoy the lifestyle that you really want?

3   How much risks are you willing to take? As you grow older, you must take on lesser risks. The reason is that your chance of recovering from a failure diminishes too. *Mahirap nang makabangon kung tayo ay madadapa lalo't kung may edad na.* The amount of risks you can take will help you decide whether you should be aggressive, conservative, reasonable and prudent, or flexible in your approach to investing.

4   What level of financial comfort do you want to have in the next three years, five years, ten years? *Ano ang importante sa iyo sa bawat yugto ng buhay mo?* Set your goal accordingly. For example, you might decide to prioritize your children's education. In the next three to five years, your primary goal should be to save enough money to finance their education.

5   How and by how much can you augment your current income? Think about the sidelines and small businesses that you can get into so you can have additional active income while you are still in the start-up phase.

6   How much can you afford to save monthly? *Magkano ba talaga ang kaya mong itabi buwan-buwan?* Is it 5%, 10%, or 20% of your current income?

7   Which among your current expenses can you do without? Remember most expenses are OPTIONAL. *Marami tayong* *gastos na hindi naman talagang kailangan para mabuhay.*

8 For OFWs reading this book, a good question to ask yourself is this: How soon do I want to come home for good? *Kailan ko gustong "mag-for good na"?* How much assets and investments should I have to be able to do it?

9 After considering all the above questions, you should be ready to determine how much Net Worth (Total Assets minus Total Liabilities), you should have at the end of each life phase. It would be advisable to adjust this target every three to five years. *Nag-iiba ang ating mga layunin sa pagdaan ng panahon at sa bawat yugto ng ating buhay.*

In trying to answer these questions, try to consult with knowledgeable professionals.

> *Inuulit-ulit ko na kailangan*
> *tayong magtanong*
> *sa talagang marunong*
> *at nakaaalam.*

After you have gone over the questions above, you should be about ready to set your financial goals.

Setting financial goals is like dreaming your dreams. It is like imagining your wants and describing them to yourself in terms of what, when and how much. *Anu-ano pa ang pangarap mo at papaano mo ito makakamit?*

But being a human endeavor, setting goals must follow certain rules of success:

:Q: **First rule:** Put it in writing. *Isulat!*

There was a study made in a U.S. university where they surveyed graduating students on what their plans and goals were. Of those surveyed, 97% had no written plans. Only 3% had written plans. Twenty years later, they looked at the personal and financial net worth of the same people who were surveyed twenty years before and their findings were very revealing. The net worth of the 3% who had written goals were much greater than the 97% who had no written plans.

Ito ay nagpapatunay na ang nakasulat na mga tunguhin ay mas naisasagawa kaysa mga planong nananatili lang sa isip.

"Until you commit your goals to paper, you have intentions that are seeds without soil."

Anonymous

:Q: **Second rule:** State it in positive terms.

For example: I will save PhP 5,000 every payday so I can buy a house in 15 years. This is more effective than saying I will not spend too much on entertainment. People tend to achieve their goals if they look at them as a specific target to achieve. Stating goals positively is an effective way to ensure their achievement.

Kailangang may particular na layunin at hindi 'yung nasa alapaap lamang.

Third rule: Set a specific timetable for each goal.

Goals without target dates of achievement will remain as pure wants. They promote procrastination because commitment will not be firm.

Magpapabukas-bukas tayo kapag walang
nakatakda na araw, buwan o taon
ang ating tunguhin.

 Fourth rule: Monitor progress.

Monitoring progress assures achievement, particularly when progress is being seen and felt. Positive developments always inject confidence and increase the capacity of the person to ensure eventual achievement of the goal. Remember that winning is a habit and seeing continued progress will lead to developing positive habits that spell success.

Maglaan tayo ng oras buwan-buwan
o taun-taon para magrepaso kung nasaan na tayo
sa ating panaginip. Kapag tayo ay umaasenso,
lalo na tayong gaganahang mag-sumikap at
madadagdagan ang ating kakayahan.

91

You can do it. *Kaya mo 'to!*

- Do some soul-searching on what you really want as your financial goal.

  Intindihin mo ang iyong tunay na hangarin tungkol sa iyong kalagayang pinansyal.

- As you do this, write it down following what you have learned in this book.

  Isulat mo ang iyong layuning pinansyal batay sa natutunan mo sa librong ito.

- Review your financial condition and your goal every month or at least every year.

  Buwan-buwan o di kaya taun-taon, suriin ang iyong kalagayang pinansyal at kung nasaan ka na hambing sa iyong layunin. Alamin kung ang iyong netong halaga (net worth) ay lumago o nabawasan.

Part 2

What You Can Do

CHAPTER 10

Ksk Commandments For Financial Freedom

Organize your financial plans for easy reference and quick review.

ORGANIZE your financial plans for easy reference. Your financial plans are by no means permanent. You need to review them regularly.

After you've determined your financial targets, I would also advise you to start putting your financial files in order. You need to place all important documents in their respective folders. You would need folders for the following:

- **Financial Statements**

  This will contain your regularly update SAL and PIES.

- **Cash**

  This should contain bank statements and a ledger for your expenses and disbursements.

- **Insurance and Medical Policies**

  Must contain the actual policies and the name and contact details of the agent and all the important telephone numbers that you need to call in case of an emergency.

- **Pre-need Plans**

  Must contain the actual policies and the name and contact details of the agent and all the important telephone numbers.

- **Assets**

  Must contain a list of all your significant physical assets such as house and lot, cars, and jewelry, categorized whether fully paid or not.

- **Utilities**

  Must include all electric, telephone, mobile phone, water bills.

- **Household Expenses**

  A ledger containing your entire household expenses, such as groceries, salaries of helpers, among other expenses. This should include all payment schedules for very important commitments such as premiums and/or loans payable to insurance, banks and preneed companies.

- **Entertainment**
  Include all expenses for dining-out, watching movies, and/or gifts.
- **Miscellaneous Expenses**
  This should contain all others not covered above.

Nasasa-iyo na kung gaanong katagal mong gustong itago ang mga papeles na inayos mo.

Ang mga importante tulad ng titulo, plano at insurance policies ay dapat nakalagay sa ligtas na lugar. Mas mabuti kung ito ay nasa "safety deposit box" ng bangko o "fire-resistant safe" sa bahay mo.

Ang mga resibo ay maaari nang itapon pagkaraan ng anim na buwan o isang taon depende sa iyong pagkalista ng mga ito.

Siguraduhin mo lang na alam ng isa mong tunay na pinagkakatiwalaan kung nasaan ang mga importanteng papeles mo kung sakaling may mangyari sa iyo.

You are ready to set your financial goal now that you already know where you are financially. However, before you begin setting your financial goal, it is important to study and practice the principles in the following chapters.

Steps to Financial Freedom come next.

Mga Hakbang Patungo sa Kalayaan sa Kakapusan ang susunod.

Magpatuloy sa pagbabasa. Marami pang mga paksa ang ating pag-uusapan!

You can do it. *Kaya mo 'to!*

- Organize and maintain your financial files in order. Have separate files for your cash disbursements, assets, pre-need pension and academic plans, or insurance plans and other important documents with clear relevance to your personal financial statements. It is easier to review your financial goals if you have your documents readily accessible.

Ihiwalay at ayusin ang mga papeles mong pinansyal sa isang kahon o kabinet. Siguraduhin na ang lahat ng mga impormasyon at record hinggil sa salaping kinikita o ginagastos ay maayos na nakatabi. Mas madali kang makapagsusuri muli kung ang mga papeles ay kumpleto at nasa ayos.

CHAPTER 11

KsK Commandment #1 - Pay yourself first

*Savings is an expense
that buys your future.*

You are your First Source of Capital

WHERE WILL I get my capital to generate investment income?

For most of us, our major source of capital is our active income from salary, allowance, overtime and maybe some form of "sideline". A portion of this active income must be dedicated to savings that will generate investment income.

Sa umpisa, mahirap maisip kung paano lalago ang ating pera kung active income lang ang ating kinikita. Ngunit kung makapagtatabi ka ng savings mula sa active income mo, darating ang panahon na magkakaroon kayo ng sabay na active at passive income. Ito ang lalong magpapalago ng inyong maiipon.

However, as an aside, our own ideas could serve as our capital and should not be ignored. Intellectual capital is today the source of great wealth in developed countries. Look at Bill Gates, the founder of Microsoft. He is the richest man in the world today and his starting capital was his brains. He produced a powerful idea, which the whole world today is paying for. His "Windows" operating system is used in more than 70% of all personal computers in the world. All around us today, we see entrepreneurs starting with simple ideas that end up becoming multi-billion ventures like Jollibee, Splash, Max's, etc.

Kung mayroon kayong henyo at ideya na naiiba, kailangan ninyo itong gamitin.

If you want to achieve financial freedom you have to start saving NOW! This is the most critical part of your journey to financial independence. You must set aside a portion of your earnings as savings before you start paying for your expenses.

Most of us define SAVINGS as

INCOME less EXPENSES

=

SAVINGS.

This is a very wrong definition! *Maling-mali!*

INCOME
less
SAVINGS
=
EXPENSE

Ang dapat...

Always remember that SAVINGS IS REALLY AN EXPENSE! It is, however, an EXPENSE that BUYS YOUR FUTURE.

Most of us who are employed look at our salary purely as our personal income. Almost automatically, we look at our income (salary) as ours to spend for our living and other desirable expenses.

Dapat tingnan natin ang ating sarili na parang isang korporasyon. Sa korporasyon, laging may plano at badyet. Hindi maaaring gumasta kung salungat sa plano at badyet.

What is the first expense priority of a business?

Ang suweldo ng mga empleyado ay ang pinakaimportanteng gastusin ng isang korporasyon.

If you agree with this, shouldn't your first priority be then paying yourself first, being the sole employee of your own "company"?

Paying yourself in this instance means compensating yourself for the "use" of an income-generating asset, which is yourself.

This compensation should be the first priority in the disbursement of your salary for the living expenses of the family. More specifically, this first charge to your salary should be allocated to fund your needs in the future when you can no longer work. This compensation is your savings and it is your primary source of capital.

> *Ang pinakaimportanteng ari-arian mo*
> *ay ang iyong sarili. Kaya dapat ang sarili mo*
> *ang una mong babayaran.*
> *Pagkatapos mong mabayaran ang sarili mo*
> *para ikaw ay makapag-impok, saka ka pa lamang*
> *maglalaan ng iyong panggastos.*

Thus your income must first be reduced by your savings needs. What is left after is then available for living expenses.

Inuulit ko, if you seriously look at your expenses, you will find that most of these expenses are optional. *Karamihan sa gastos ay opsyonal o hindi kailangan!* That is why if you immediately set aside up to 20% of your regular income as savings, you will more likely find out that you can really live with a budget of no more than 80% of your regular income.

Most of the families I talk to have one expense item that is common to all, entertainment expense. These are expenses for eating out, snacks, movies, magazines and so many other useless purchases like fashion items. These expenses are almost always spent on impulse especially when the family goes "malling."

Entertainment expenses are really optional.

Opkors, kailangan naman may libangan tayo. Ngunit maari naman tayong pumili ng libreng libangan o di kaya 'yung mas mura. Minsan nga 'yung libre o mas murang libangan ang mas masaya dahil alam mo na nakakaimpok ka na bukod pa sa nasisiyahan ka.

Para hindi ka matukso sa paggasta nang higit sa iyong kakayanan, kailangan may badyet ka para sa linggu-lingg o buwan-buwan. At ito ay dapat din repasuhin bago pumasok ang susunod na linggo o susunod na buwan.

Parang mahirap ito ngunit ito ay sa umpisa lang. Kapag nakasanayan mo ay hahanap-hanapin mo na ang iyong notbuk na pinagsusulatan.

KEEP REGULAR LISTS OF ALL YOUR EXPENSES TO HELP YOU STAY WITHIN YOUR BUDGET.

More often, as you go down your list of expenses, you will find that you are making interest payments on credit card debts. It is so common among employees to˚ rack up credit card debt to fund their impulse buying. Before they know it, they end up being so much in debt that they can afford to pay only for the interest charges.

Credit card debt is probably the most expensive debt you can incur. Credit card companies might charge an average of three to four percent per month. Because of this high interest rate, I also advise you to pay off credit card debt and other high-interest consumer loans before you start saving for other things.

Mr. & Mrs. A like to eat out

Mr. & Mrs. A have a net total household income of almost PhP 60,000 per month. They told me that, although they have only .two young children, and their rent is only PhP 8,000 per month, they seem to always run out of money. Their expenses almost always take up their entire income. If they happen to have any medical or any kind of unplanned emergency expense, they end up borrowing from friends or relatives.

I suggested that they record their daily expenses for one month and to let me know what the results are. I wasn't surprised when they "discovered" that they were spending almost PhP 12,000 every month on eating out and going to the malls. I asked them what assets or goods they got in return. The answer was none. All that money went to consumption.

Mr. & Mrs. A were spending twenty percent (20%) of their income on useless things and they were not even aware of it! A clear example that expenses are almost always optional and unnecessary. I did not look into the other expenses of the couple but I am almost sure they financed most of those unnecessary expenses with their credit card. If they did, I just hope that they paid their credit card bill on time. Credit card debt is the most expensive debt next to "five-six".

A lesson on savings

When Ms. S arrived in Hong Kong 14 years ago, in 1990, to work as a domestic helper, one of her main objectives was to learn how to be more prudent in handling her finances. Ms. S was earning enough back in Manila. But being young and single, she would always end up spending her money on worthless things. She enjoyed life as much as she could. She was, in her own words, a *"gastadora."*

Her parents were really not expecting her to be able to save a substantial amount because they knew all about her not-so-wise spending habits. So they were pleasantly surprised when about a year ago she showed them her bank accounts and her properties. The documents showed that she then had a net worth of PhP 3.4 million.

How was she able to accumulate that much? For most domestic helpers who earn only between HK$ 3,000 and 4,500 a month, it seems that such a feat is impossible. But Ms. S has proven that it is not. She is still working in Hong Kong, but only because she wants to and not anymore because she needs to.

Her journey to financial independence picked up after she noticed that the value of the peso had been steadily declining. This observation firmed up her belief that she should save only in US dollars. It was a personal choice that paid off very well. Every time she had some money, she would convert it to US dollars before depositing it in the bank. It became her goal to save at least US$ 2,000 at the end of every contract term which was usually good for 2 years.

She became conscious about her spending habits. She would prepare a monthly budget. She would send money back home but she made it clear to her family that she could not provide more than what they really needed. She never gave in every time there was a request for money that she thought was unnecessary. Her family thought she just did not have any money because they still believed that she had not changed her spending habits.

Every chance she could, she would also invest in residential lots in good subdivisions in her hometown in Ilo-ilo. There were several instances when she was asked to continue paying for the amortization of lots that were bought by friends and family members, giving her the opportunity to buy properties at less than their market value. Today, she has several good residential lots in her name that she intends to sell once she is ready to retire.

Through her experience she learned that it is never too late to start planning one's financial future. She was already 30 years old when she decided to take hold of her financial future by saving and spending her money wisely. "No matter how many mistakes you may have committed in the past, it is still possible to change," she said.

Nakatutuwa si Ms. S. Ginagamit niya ang karamihan ng mga prinsipyong pinag-uusapan sa librong ito. Kahit marami na siyang alam, nakikinig pa rin siya sa aking payo at pumupunta siya sa aking seminar. Siguradong lalong makatutulong ito sa kaniya pagdating ng panahon.

Ang payo ko lamang sa inyong mga gustong gumaya kay Ms. S, mag-ingat sa basta pagbili ng mga lupain. Katulad ni Ms. B sa Chapter Three, baka mawalan ito ng tunay na halaga kung ito ay wala namang kita.

SAVINGS is your first source of capital.

You can do it. *Kaya mo 'to!*

- Pay yourself first and save a portion of what you paid yourself.

  Sa pagtanggap ng iyong sahod, itabi mo ang para sa iyong sarili. Ibukod mo rin ang iyong iipunin na pang puhunan sa darating na panahon.

- Spend your money wisely. Keep a list of your expenses and you might discover that so much is spent on useless items.

  Maging matalino sa paggamit ng iyong salapi. Isulat lahat ng iyong gastusin at baka matuklasan mo kung ano ang pinagkakagastahan mo na walang silbi.

CHAPTER 12

KsK Commandment # 2 - Define your financial target at each life phase

*Base your goal on
your financial phase.*

YOUR FINANCIAL GOAL must be based on whatever phase in life you are in financially. A person who is still in the Start-up Phase cannot have the same goal as someone already in the Asset Allocation phase. Determine what your needs and wants are. As you advance into retirement, you should be able to have sufficient passive income that will provide for not only your needs but your wants as well.

Napag-usapan natin ito sa Chapters 2, 5 at 6
ngunit importante na bigyang-diin ang mga
alituntunin sa Start-up Phase sapagkat ito ang unang
layunin natin. Sa mga susunod na aklat natin tatalakayin
ang ibang Life Phases.

At the Start-up Phase most of your income would be used for basic needs. Apart from food, clothing and shelter you have the obligation to set aside money (Savings) for the following:

- Cash reserves or emergency fund
- Term insurance
- Medical/Income Insurance
- Savings or Pension or Investment Plan

Ideally, you need to have cash reserves sufficient to cover your expenses for the next six months in case you lose your job. Six months should be enough for you to find a new job.

You need to get sufficient insurance coverage to ensure that, in case anything happens to you, you would still be able to provide for your family's basic needs. As you and the members of your family grow older, your need for insurance protection decreases.

For example, a 30-year-old head of the family with two kids in grade school would need more insurance coverage than a 50-year-old head of the family whose kids are already professionals. Because of this, it is more prudent to get term insurance instead of the ordinary life insurance policy.

Shown below is how this savings rule is applied. This example is based on the income and expenses of Marilou Santos whom we introduced in Chapter Two.

● Fundamental Savings Rule: 20% of gross regular monthly income (GRMI).

● How should savings be distributed:

  ● CASH RESERVES (10% of GRMI per month)

  ● TERM LIFE INSURANCE: Cover yourself with at least three years' worth of primary income.

  ● MEDICAL HOSPITAL INSURANCE

  ● LONG-TERM SAVINGS PLANS such as:
    Housing, Pension, Education and the like.

The rules on insurance are further clarified in subsequent sections.

Marilou Santos: Savings Plan (In PhP):

Gross Monthly Income (GRMI):	35,900
20% Target Savings	7,180
Savings Distribution:	

Cash Reserves (10% of GRMI)	3,590
(Stop after accumulating amount equal to 6 months GRMI, or PhP215,400)	

Term Insurance: Coverage should be
3 yrs Income or PhP1,080,000. (Premium
cost is PhP7 per year or PhP 0.58 per
month per PhP1,000 worth of insurance)   630

Medical Hospital Insurance:
30 days' benefit at PhP1,000 per day;
(Premium cost is Php50 per month)   50

Available for LONG TERM savings plans:
Target Savings LESS savings allocated to
Cash reserves and all insurance coverages:
7,180 LESS 4,270 (3,590+630+50)   2,910

Now try and rewrite your own income and expense
statement providing for immediate savings before your living
expenses. For your reference, Marilou Santos rewrote hers.
Her revised PIES is presented below:

MARILOU SANTOS
PERSONAL STATEMENT OF INCOME & EXPENSE (Based on KSK
Principles and in PhP)
Salary HK$4,200 = Php 30,000 per month

Gross Monthly Income	35,900
ACTIVE:	
Primary: Sahod	30,000
Additional (Sidelines)	5,600
PASSIVE: SECONDARY	
Interest income	300
Other Income (Lupa)	0

Savings

1. Cash Reserves	3,590	
2. Term Insurance	630	
3. Hospital Income Insurance	50	
4. Long Term Savings (Pension; other investments; housing)	2,910	
TOTAL SAVINGS		7,180

BUDGET FOR LIVING EXPENSES		28,720
Food (Pamalengke at Groceries)	9,000	
Renta sa bahay	0	
Gastos sa bahay (ex. Gasul, etc)	1,000	
Pamasahe	1,500	
Cellphone	1,500	
Kuryente	1,500	
Tubig	500	
Allowance-"Baon ng mga bata"	2,000	
Eskwelahan	1,000	
LIVING EXPENSES		18,000

R & R (OPTIONAL EXPENSES)		
-movies/"pasyal"	800	
-clothes/personal (etc)	600	
Babasahin	200	
Biglaan gastos (Gifts, etc)	200	
TOTAL: OPTIONAL EXPENSES		1,800

OTHER CASH PAYMENTS		
House Amortization	3,375	
Credit cards	1,660	
Other personal debts	2,000	
Pension plans	1,880	
TOTAL: OTHER CASH PMTS		8,915
TOTAL MONTHLY EXPENSES		28,715

NET CASH AVAILABLE for Additional Investments (e.g. for debt reduction & others)		5

Sa PIES na ito, bukod pa sa naitabing 20% ni Marilou, mayroon pa siyang PhP 5 na pwede pa ring idagdag sa savings niya. Ang punto dito ay kung may karagdagang kita si Marilou, lahat na ito ay pwedeng ilagak sa iba pang mga investment.

A Note on Emergencies

We have to discuss emergency funds because emergencies happen.

Hospitalization Insurance should cover medical emergencies. If you can afford to cover your close relatives who depend on you with Hospitalization Insurance, this would be ideal.

You can buy one memorial plan or cremation plan in case someone who depends on you dies and you have to pay for the funeral. This is transferable. If it was used, you can buy a new one.

For all kinds of emergencies, especially non-life threatening emergencies, it is best that you stay calm and not spend all your savings. Do not be hasty in offering all your savings.

Suriing mabuti ang pagkalubha ng emergency at maghanap ng ibang paraan na makatutulong. Malamang hindi yan ang huling emergency at kailangang mayroon ka pang natitira para sa kinabukasan.

Kung magasta mo ang iyong naimpok, kailangan kang mag-"double time" sa iyong paghahanap ng ipapalit. Mawawala pati ang interes ng iyong naimpok at tuluyan ding mababawasan ang iyong "passive income".

Kung kaya mong mag-impok ng higit sa 20% para makapaghanda sa emergency, lalong mabuti.

You can do it. *Kaya mo 'to!*

- Accept your "Life Stage" and set your financial goal based on where you are.

  Intindihin ang iyong layuning pinansyal para maisaayos ang iyong mga tunguin batay sa iyong "Life Stage."

- Save at least 20% of gross regular monthly income.

  Itabi ang 20% ng iyong kita buwan-buwan.

- 10% or half of your 20% initial savings, should go to Cash Reserves/Emergency Fund. You should have Cash Reserves equivalent to six months salary in case you lose your job.

  Ilaan ang 10% sa "Cash Reserves/Emergency Fund". Kinakailangan may "Cash Reserves" ka na ang katumbas ay higit sa anim na buwang kita. Ito ang gagamitin mo kung saka-sakaling mawalan ka ng trabaho.

- The other 10% should be used to pay for Term Insurance. Medical/Hospital income Insurance, Savings or Pension or Investment Plan. You must only buy these from reputable companies.

  Bumili ka ng "Term o Medical/Hospital income Insurance at Savings o Pension o Investment Plan" mula sa mga matatag na kumpanya lamang.

- In case of emergencies, understand the situation. Do not be hasty in offering all your savings.

  Hangga't maaari, huwag gastusin ang lahat ng iyong naimpok hangga't hindi mo nasusuri ang tunay na kalubhaan ng "emergency".

CHAPTER 13

KsK Commandment #3 - Stop spending on things that decline in value

Base your goal on your financial phase.

WHEN YOU START analyzing your PIES, chances are you will realize you have spent a large sum of money on a lot of things that eventually lose in value. I notice that many of us buy appliances, furniture and gadgets that we can otherwise do without. We think these things are assets but they are not. You should stop buying on impulse. Before you buy, ask yourself if you really need it or whether or not you can really afford it.

Know the difference between asset and liability. If you religiously update your SAL, you will find out whether or not your expenditures are increasing your Net Worth or not. If not, you probably have been buying liabilities more than assets. Robert Kiyosaki says: "Assets put money in your pocket. Liabilities take out money from your pocket."

Assets … Liabilities

If you are a salesman, is a car an asset or a liability?

Most of you will answer that it is an asset. Why? Because as a salesman, you need a car to move around, call on new customers, and also to look for new ones. In principle, this answer is correct. But in personal finance, it may not be correct. When then is it financially correct? And when is it wrong?

Mr. G buys a Pajero

Mr. G, a real estate salesman, immediately bought a Pajero when he earned a huge commission after selling a house worth PhP 30 million. He earned a commission of PhP 900,000 in less than one week. He put a PhP 600,000 down payment and agreed to pay almost PhP 26,000 per month for 3 years. The real estate market slowed down and Mr. G was no longer able to sell regularly. The time came when he no longer had the income to pay the PhP 26,000 monthly amortization. He still had two (2) years to go. He had paid a total of PhP 912,000 by then. He tried to sell the car but after a year of usage, with the new models in the market at the same price as before, the best offer he could get was PhP 650,000 cash, and the buyer would assume thé remaining monthly amortization.

If he sold the car, he would "lose" PhP 262,000 in one year. If he did not, he would lose the total amount he had paid or PhP 912,000 since it would be re-possessed. Now, was that car an asset? Or had it become a liability? On the other hand, if he had bought instead a simple car worth, let us say PhP 500,000 he probably would not be in the bad situation he is in now. More likely, he would not need to sell it too!

If we consider the operating cost of that Pajero for one year, he probably spent another PhP 8,000 per month for insurance, fuel and maintenance. This was an additional PhP 96,000 cost for just one year. Clearly, his decision to buy that Pajero was not a financially sound decision.

Rich in assets?

Mrs. O is a part-time writer. She claims that whenever she has extra cash, she buys valuable items like antiques and jewelry. She says she does this because she believes these are items that always appreciate and never lose value. She does not have updated financial records or appraisal of all these items she has accumulated so far.

When I asked her how much these valuables have appreciated over the years, she could not give an answer. It seems that she has no real basis yet for determining whether her investments are up or down compared to her purchase price. She just feels that she has assets that are valuable. I also asked whether she has made money in actually selling any valuable jewelry that she has. Again, it seems she has not really been selling any except once when she needed cash for traveling. In that instance, she had to sell one of her jewelry pieces at a loss. She says she had no choice because she was in a hurry.

This is again a typical case where wealth is in the form of assets that have no clear exchange value and no real liquidity. In the event that Mrs. O will get into a serious need for cash, she will most likely end up again selling one or more of her valuables at a loss.

Mrs. O fortunately is not hard up. She is very rich in such assets. But is she really growing her net worth?

Very likely, if Mrs. O had placed her cash in government securities and just rolled the interest earnings, she would have accumulated a much higher cash value for her investments. And she would see true growth in her net worth.

Sabi niya mas mabuti naman na bumili siya
ng mga alahas kaysa mga mamahaling damit
at sapatos na talagang nawawalan ng halaga
at hindi uli naipagbibili kundi
sa "garage sale". Totoo rin ito!

Ngunit ang alahas ay napakapersonal.
Ang maganda at mamahalin para sa iyo
ay maaaring hindi kasing ganda at mamahalin
sa tingin ng iba. Kapag bumili ka ng alahas,

dapat talagang kaya ng iyong badyet at para sa iyo at hindi para "investment". Kung maipagbili mo at kumita ka, swerte na lang yon. Iba namang usapan kung ikaw naman ay alahera na nangangalakal o nagba-"buy and sell" ng alahas.

Some women buy and sell jewelry. Some buy and keep jewelry for investment. They believe that the value of jewelry over time will grow faster than other types of investment. Both cases may be correct. Both could also be wrong. What will make it right or wrong is the personal financial situation of the investor. Buying and selling jewelry can be good business if you have a real market and know what items to sell. You should also know how to protect yourself from the risks of non-payment, theft, swindlers and the like. On the other hand, if you invest in jewelry, and you do not have sufficient resources, you may just end up being forced to sell your jewelry at a loss when you need cash badly and you don't have any other asset except your jewelry. The principle behind it is simple. The value of any asset depends upon what the owner can do with it. Ultimately, the disposition of any asset has to result in an increase in personal net worth. Otherwise, it is a liability.

*Ang halaga ng isang bagay, maging alahas
o ano pa mang ari-arian, ay nabibigyan ng
katuturan kung ang may-ari nito ay mayroong
pakinabang sa bagay na ito. Ang isang toneladang
ginto na nasa ilalim ng dagat ay walang halaga
sa bayan. Subalit kung ito ay nasa ibabaw
ng lupa at nasa ating pangangalaga,
kahit ito ay iilan-ilang onsa, ito ay may halaga
at maipagpapalit ng salapi.*

You can do it. *Kaya mo 'to!*

- Do not buy things that lose value.

  *Iwasan ang pagbili ng gamit
  na nawawalan nang halaga.*

- Do not buy on impulse.

  Isipin at aralin bago bumili ng anuman.

- Increase your Assets. Assets give you money. Decrease your Liabilities. Liabilities take money away from you.

  *Dagdagan ang iyong ari-arian. Ito ay nagbibigay sa
  iyo ng pera. Bawasan ang iyong utang.
  Ito ay nagbabawas ng iyong pera.*

- If you regularly update your SAL, you will know if your spending is increasing your Net Worth or not.

  *Kung buwan-buwan o taun-taon sinusuri mo ang iyong
  SAL, malalaman mo kung lumalaki ang buong
  kahalagahan mo.*

CHAPTER 14

KsK Commandment # 4 Protect your greatest income generating asset, YOURSELF

Protecting yourself should be your first priority.

YOUR GREATEST INCOME generator is yourself. Protecting yourself should always be your priority.

Insurance

Your family depends on your ability to generate income. They will suffer a serious financial loss if you are no longer able to generate income for them. Therefore, it is important to cover yourself with insurance. Insurance is needed only when there is a possibility of unbearable financial loss.

The important question however is: How much and what kind of insurance do you need?

How much insurance?

The amount of insurance you need depends on who would suffer financially in case you died. It will also depend on how much of your income your family is dependent on. For example, if you have no children and your income is the sole source of funding for you and your spouse's living expenses, then you should acquire insurance to cover that amount that your spouse will need to live on while he or she is looking for another source of income (or possibly a replacement for you) in case you die or are no longer around. How much that will be depends on how much time you will give him or her to recover from losing you. Is it going to be three, four, five or ten years? The longer the time, the higher the amount of insurance needed.

If your spouse will need PhP 300,000 per year to survive and you decide to give him or her three years "recovery" time because he or she is still young and will not have difficulty in finding new sources of income (or your replacement), then you need to buy insurance at only three times PhP 300,000 or PhP 900,000.

What kind of insurance?

Because you should just be concerned with pure protection, the most practical types of insurance you can buy are:

● Term Life - These are life policies that you pay premium for year to year. There are no cash values. The benefits are only paid out to your beneficiaries only when you die.

- Accident - Similar to term, your benefits are paid out only if you are injured or killed in an accident.

- Medical and/or Hospital Income - Hospital income insurance is the simplest form of medical insurance. You buy specific amounts of benefits for every day you get to be hospitalized. Normally, the benefits are given as a fixed amount per day for one month per year.

These are the most economical types of insurance you can buy. They are particularly affordable if the policy is bought on a group account basis, i.e. the insured is a member of an organization that secures the insurance policy. The premium rates are more reasonable and these types are most suitable for protection coverage. These protection measures are so affordable that you must make sure you are covered. Most people buy more insurance than needed because of the so-called future savings built into the insurance policy. Generally, this feature makes your life insurance policy cost more than what you really need.

There are many variations on the types of insurance mentioned above. You should consult with reputable brokers and insurance companies for specific terms and prices of these insurance coverages.

Physical health

While you prepare yourself for adversities through insurance coverage, I cannot over-emphasize the need to keep yourself physically healthy. You must eat a balanced diet and reduce junk food intake. Have enough hours of sleep.

It is ideal to exercise. However, if you do not have the luxury of time, there are many ways to convert your daily chores into exercise. For example,

 Use the stairs instead of the elevator.

 Walk briskly.

 Instead of riding a vehicle for short distances, walk.

 Get out of the vehicle a few blocks away from your destination and walk.

 While cleaning the house make every movement a chance to stretch your body.

 When riding a vehicle or while watching TV, tuck in your stomach and move your extremities to stretch.

Spiritual Health

Studies show that those who have spirituality in their life are able to endure trials and hardships much better. This must be true for us Filipinos. Despite all the setbacks in our life, we continue to smile and be happy. Ipinababahala na lang natin sa Diyos.

Tama ang magtiwala sa ating Panginoong Diyos.
Ngunit mayroon ding kasabihan:
GOD HELPS THOSE
WHO HELP THEMSELVES!

Mental health

Being so far away from home, OFWs surely feel lonely. Thus, there is the prevalent need for OFWs to band together into different associations.

However, this very bonding can be the cause of intrigues, jealousy and gossip. I think that if all OFWs just decide to focus their loneliness on improving themselves, a lot of these frustrations can be overcome. One of the ways to improvement is educating one's self.

Continuing education

That you are reading this book is already proof that you are interested in improving your knowledge.

If you have the means to take formal courses to improve your current skills or to learn new ones, you must do so. In fact, it is good to take formal courses to be able to broaden and strengthen your credentials.

Always take the opportunity to attend seminars given by experts on different areas that interest you. Even if you have to pay, if the speaker is someone you can trust, you will probably learn something to improve yourself.

Seminars that are free are big opportunities that should be considered. They also afford you the opportunity to meet like-minded individuals with whom you can network on both professional and personal bases. However, you must realize that when a seminar is free, most of the participants do not give it their full attention.

When you participate in a seminar, make the most of it! Whether or not you pay, give it your full attention. Otherwise, leave the venue permanently if the topic does not interest you after all, or if you prefer to talk to your friend. It is unfair to the other participants and to the speaker to disturb their concentration by carrying on another conversation while the lecturer is speaking.

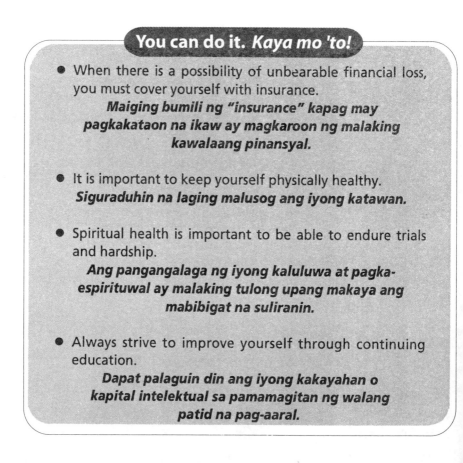

You can do it. *Kaya mo 'to!*

- When there is a possibility of unbearable financial loss, you must cover yourself with insurance.
  Maiging bumili ng "insurance" kapag may pagkakataon na ikaw ay magkaroon ng malaking kawalaang pinansyal.

- It is important to keep yourself physically healthy.
  Siguraduhin na laging malusog ang iyong katawan.

- Spiritual health is important to be able to endure trials and hardship.
  Ang pangangalaga ng iyong kaluluwa at pagka-espirituwal ay malaking tulong upang makaya ang mabibigat na suliranin.

- Always strive to improve yourself through continuing education.
  Dapat palaguin din ang iyong kakayahan o kapital intelektual sa pamamagitan ng walang patid na pag-aaral.

KsK Commandment # 5 - Grow with the economy and beat inflation.

Money is an ever-declining value.

YOU MUST ALWAYS remember that you are working against time and money.

You have to make sure that your investments earn more than the inflation rate. Today's inflation rate is 4-5%. You should plan to earn more than 5% on your investments. Your investments or savings should produce passive income at a rate more than 5%. It is not enough that you start saving. You also have to consider where you are putting your money. Your savings and investments should always generate an income that is higher than the inflation rate.

Estimate your desired net worth upon retirement.

One way to plan for your financial future, given the reality of inflation is to make projections of how much your net worth should be by the time you retire.

Ang pag-aaral kung papaano palalaguin ang puhunan na galing sa naimpok upang makaabot sa sapat na halaga pagdating ng panahon ng pagretiro ay maaaring isagawa alinsunod sa ganitong proseso:

 Alamin ang "inflation rate" bawat taon. Ito ang batayan kung magkano ang magiging halaga ng piso mo pagdating ng iyong pagretiro sa edad na 65. Sa ngayong panahon, maaring gamitin ang 5%.

 Batay sa edad mo ngayon, alamin mo kung ilang taon pa bago ka umabot sa edad na 65.

Alamin mo ang "future value" ng kinikita mo ngayon pag ikaw ay 65 na batay sa implasyon na 5%. Ang halagang iyan ang dapat na maging "passive income" mo taun-taon pag retiro mo.

Halimbawa, kung ang interes na kaya mong kitain taun-taon ay 10%. Ang dapat mong mabuo na "net worth" sa edad na 65 ay yung halaga na kung kumita ng 10% ay makapagbibigay ng kita na kasing halaga ng "passive income" na kababanggit lang natin. Tingnan natin ito sa mga sumusunod na halimbawa.

Ang pundamental na tugunin ng bawat isa ay makaipon o makabuo ng "personal net worth" na makapagbibigay ng "passive income" na kayang tustusin ang mga gastusin sa antas na pamumuhay na iyong pinili.

Let us say that you are 20 years of age. You are earning PhP 130,000 per year (PhP 10,000 per month) and you want to maintain your purchasing power at this income when you retire at age 65.

To be able to retire with the same purchasing power upon retirement, you should know the equivalent of your present income at age 65. This amount is what your net worth or earning assets should be earning at that time. Your plan, therefore, is to build up your net worth to this amount over the years before retirement.

At 5% inflation rate, the equivalent of your present annual earnings of PhP 130,000 is PhP 1,168,050 at age 65.

At an earnings rate of 10% per annum, your Earning Assets should be PhP 11,680,500. This means that by the time you retire, you should have PhP 11,680,500 in cash and/or earning assets. This should be your minimum net worth.

Case 1: If you start saving at 20 years of age, YOU HAVE 45 YEARS TO ACHIEVE IT!

You will only need to save PhP 1,114 per month till you reach the age of 65 to accumulate PhP 11,680,500. This is just like saving 11% of your PhP 10,000 current monthly income. Surely,

133

your monthly income will increase sooner or later. If this happens, you will have more money to save, thus making it possible for you to achieve your target net worth even before you reach the age of 65.

Case 2: What if you start saving only at 30 years of age when you are earning PhP 260,000 per year (PhP 20,000 per month).

To be able to retire with the same purchasing power upon retirement that you wanted at age 20, (PhP 1,168,050) YOU ONLY HAVE 35 YEARS TO SAVE PhP 11,680,500!

If your savings earn 10% per year, you now need to save PhP 3,080 per month till you reach the age of 65 to accumulate PhP 11,680,500. This is equivalent to saving 15% of your PhP 20,000 monthly income.

Case 3: What if you start saving only at 40 years of age when you are earning PhP 520,000 per year (PhP 40,000 per month).

To be able to retire with the same purchasing power upon retirement that you wanted at age 20, (PhP 1,168,050) YOU THEN ONLY HAVE 25 YEARS TO SAVE PhP 11,680,500!

Based on an earning rate of 10% per year, you will need to save PhP 8,800 per month till you reach the age of 65 to accumulate PhP 11,680,500. Because you have delayed saving and you only have 25 years to grow your money, you will now have to allocate 22% of your monthly income of PhP 40,000.

Table 1: EFFECT OF DELAYING SAVINGS

Present Age	Current Monthly Salary	Current Yearly Salary	Target Earning Assets by Retirement Age 65 years	Years to Reach Earning Assets Goal	Monthly Savings	% of Current Salary
	PhP	PhP	PhP		PhP	
20 yrs.	10,000	130,000	11,680,500	45 years	1,114	11%
30 yrs.	20,000	260,000	11,680,500	35 years	3,080	15%
40 yrs.	40,000	520,000	11,680,500	25 years	8,800	22%

Table 1 again shows the importance of saving early. By saving early, you can enjoy the years of your life when you are still physically strong and have more opportunities. At the same time, you know that it takes less savings to prepare for your retirement.

Malaking ginhawa ang nakapag-ipon ng maaga.
Habang kaya pa ng katawan mo, maaari ka nang
magsaya sapagkat alam mo na mayroon
ka nang nakalaan para sa iyong pagreretiro.

Historical performance of Philippine Financial Assets

Now that you know how much net worth to build up to, you should look at investment options that can beat inflation. This discussion is detailed in Chapter 19 under KSK Commandment number 9 (Invest and Diversify). For now, let me tell you what actually happened in the Philippine Financial Markets from January 1987 through December 2000. Here you will be pleased to know that you can beat inflation without taking undue risks.

In our economy, there are classes of financial assets available to ordinary income earners. If you invested PhP 10,000 in January of 1987 in these various financial assets, you would have grown this investment to the following amounts by the end of December 2000. Inflation rate over this 14-year period averaged 9.34%:

Table 2*		
Comparative Growth Rates of Financial Assets		
Jan 1987 - Dec 2000		
Asset Class	Ave After tax % Return per yr	Value of PhP10,000 at end of Dec 2000
T-Bills	12.22	49,928
$ Deposit	13.06	49,885
Savings Deposits	6.83	25,172
Time Deposits	10.23	38,850
Common Stocks	14.40	17,861
INFLATION	*9.34*	*34,703*

* This information was drawn from a study of Prof. Roy Ybañez of the UP College of Business Administration on the RATES OF RETURN ON FINANCIAL ASSETS in the Philippines, 1987-2000. Note that the average annual returns on the first column refer to the yearly performance of each asset over the entire period. The terminal values on the second column simply reflect the value of a PhP 10,000 investment made in January 1987 in each asset type by the end of December 2000

Conclusions

While Table 2 is a highly simplified presentation of only one of the many findings in the study, the following conclusions are validated in the said study:

● Although the highest average return was recorded in the highly unpredictable common stock market, this was found to be the most volatile and most risky of all investments. As the Table 2 shows, because of the down market, your PhP 10,000 investment in January 1987 was only worth PhP 17,861 at the end of December 2000. In other words, this kind of investment requires full attention and competence as the values change day-to-day. The stock market can reflect good or even high average returns, but unless you, as investor, are able to choose the right stock and the right time to cash-in, you can even lose your entire principal investment.

● Except for savings deposits, all other financial assets beat inflation.

The best two investments were T-Bills and $ deposits in reputable banks. These were also the most risk-free investments. As the above table shows, you achieved an earnings rate of 12.2% beating the inflation rate of 9.34% by almost 3%. Your PhP 10,000 grew to PhP 49,928 when you only needed PhP 34,700 to keep in pace with inflation. By investing in these instruments, you not only preserved your purchasing power, you also generated additional wealth of PhP 15,228 that you can put into additional investments.

137

*Ang mga datos na nakalahad sa Table 2 sa itaas
ay nagpapakita na kaya nating talunin
ang implasyon sa pamamagitan ng maayos
at simpleng paraan na wala namang gaanong panganib.
Kung inilagak natin ang PhP 10,000 sa T-Bills noong
Enero 1987 at hinayaan natin na ito ay "mag roll"
o "mag-compound", lalago ito sa halagang PhP 49,928
pagdating ng Dec. 2000. Ang katumbas na tubo
taun-taon nito ay humigit kumulang 12.22%.
Di hamak na mas mataas ito sa implasyon noong
panahon na yon na 9.34%. Itong lamang na kinita ng T-Bills
sa implasyon na 2.86% ay nakapagbigay ng
karagdagang PhP 15,000 mula Enero 1987 hanggang
Disyembre 2000. Batay sa 9.34% implasyon, ang kasing
halaga ng PhP 10,000 noong Enero 1987
sa Disyembre 2000 ay PhP 34,703.*

The other good class of investment as shown above is US dollar deposits. Let us then take a new look at Ms. S (Chapter 11) who seems to have saved in US dollars and beat inflation at the same time.

You will recall that when Ms. S arrived in Hong Kong 14 years ago, in 1990, to work as a domestic helper, one of her main objectives was to learn how to be more prudent in handling her finances. About a year ago, her bank accounts and her properties documents showed that she now has a net worth of PhP 3.4 million.

Her story also teaches that one needs to find ways to beat inflation. In her case, she saw a perfect opportunity by saving in US dollars. There are other options available. The important thing is to know what option suits you best and have the resolve to stick to it.

You can do it. *Kaya mo 'to!*

- Make sure that your investments earn more than the inflation rate.

  Siguraduhin na ang iyong "investments" ay kumikita ng higit sa "inflation rate."

- Save early and make it easier for you to accumulate your desired net worth earlier than at age 65.

  Mag-ipon ng maaga at magiging maaga at mas madali mong maiipon ang netong halaga na angkop para sa iyong pagretiro.

- T-Bills and $ deposits in reputable banks are the most risk-free investments. From 1987 through 2000, these financial instruments are also produced the best investments returns in the Philippines.

  Ang T-Bills at $ deposits sa bangkong mapagkakatiwalaan ang pinaka-walang panganib na "investments" na pwedeng pag-lagakan ng salapi. Mula 1987 hanggang 2000, ang kita sa mga ito ang pinakamataas sa iba't ibang paraang pinansyal gaya ng "savings o time deposit" at iba pa.

CHAPTER 16

KsK Commandment # 6 - Trust the power of compound interest

*With discipline,
allow time to work for you.*

ALBERT EINSTEIN once said that man's greatest invention is compound interest. Use the power of compound interest to your advantage.

Example: If you have PhP 10,000 that earns 10% interest yearly you will be able to generate an income of PhP 1,000 per year. If you spend this PhP 1,000 interest yearly at the end of ten years you will be left with nothing but the PhP 10,000 that you started with. However, if you decide to save, instead of spend, the PhP

1,000 interest and roll it over *(ibalik sa bangko upang kumita ng interes)*, at the end of ten years your PhP 10,000 will become PhP 25,938. Even better, at the end of 15 years your PhP 10,000 will become PhP 41,772.

Similarly, if you save PhP 1 per day or PhP 30 per month, at 10% interest per year for 40 years, your money will grow to PhP166,500 compounded annually. How many of you reading this book have PhP166,500 in your bankbook today? Setting aside Php 1 per day is like giving up only two candies per day, something you don't need and is probably bad for your health too.

Work SMARTER rather than HARDER! Compound interest can make you earn four times more for the same amount of savings over the same amount of time.

For example, if you save PhP 100 per month earning 5% for 40 years, your savings will grow to PhP 152,602. If you work harder and save PhP 200 per month instead, your savings will simply double in the same forty-year period, meaning, your savings will grow to PhP 305,204.

But if you work smarter by studying and learning about other types of savings instruments, like Government Treasury Bills (T-bills) and the like, you will find out that there are long term T-Bond issues that pay out 10% or more per year. If you do that and save your PhP 100 per month by investing them in these T-bonds at 10% per year, then your PhP100-per-month savings will grow to PhP 632,408. This is FOUR (4) times the future value of the same amount of savings of PhP 100 per month at 5% over the 40-year period.

Clearly, you do not have to take unnecessary risks or "gamble" your hard-earned resources on "high-risk" investments. You only need to know how to use the power of compound interest to your advantage.

Beating inflation and growing your wealth cannot happen unless you have the will and the discipline to let time work for you. When you save and invest long term, just make sure to leave your invested money alone!

With compound interest, time and the right investment instruments, you will not need to take unnecessary risks in building up your net worth.

The story of Pepe and Pilar has been re-told over and over. Few know that Pepe and Pilar were biological twins. There is, however, an interesting anecdote about their financial lives:

> Pepe started working at the age of 18. Because of what their parents taught them about the virtue of savings, he started to save PhP 250 per month or PhP 3,000 per year while still single. He placed them in Government Retail Treasury Bills with an interest of 10% per year. He stopped saving at the age of 26 but left his savings intact and just let it grow at the rate of 10% per year compounded annually.
>
> Pilar, in the meantime, became a doctor and started to work at that same age of 26. She too started saving at the same rate of PhP 3,000 per year and invested the same in Government Treasury Bills, also earning 10% per year.

Pepe and Pilar recently retired, at the same time, at the age of 65. Who do you think has more money? Pepe or Pilar?

Pepe, from age 18 through 26, had actually set aside only PhP 24,000 by saving PhP 3,000 per year over a period of 8 years. He allowed these savings and interest income of 10% per year to compound for another 40 years until he reached age 65.

Pilar, on the other hand, had actually put aside or saved a total of PhP 120,000 with her PhP 3,000 per year over a period of 40 years, i.e., from the time she started working at age of 26 through her retirement at age 65. She also left all her savings and interest income intact and simply allowed it to compound annually.

Upon retirement, Pepe had more money than Pilar.

Through the power of compound interest, at the age of 65, Pepe's savings grew to an incredible amount of PhP 1,707,994. Pilar's savings, on the other hand, grew to only PhP 1,460,555.

HOW COULD THAT HAPPEN WHEN PILAR SAVED ALMOST FIVE TIMES MORE THAN PEPE?

The answer lies in the fact that PEPE SAVED MUCH EARLIER.

It is not how much you save but WHEN YOU START TO SAVE that determines your wealth.

You can do it. *Kaya mo 'to!*

- Be smart in saving. Using compound interest can make you earn four times more for the same amount of savings over the same period of time.

  Dapat maging listo sa pag-"invest." Alamin kung anong "investment instruments" (gaya ng "T-Bills o T-Bonds, mutual funds, etc") ang nagbibigay ng pinakamaayos na kita sa bawat pagkakataon na ikaw ay handang mag-"invest". Ang tamang pagpili ay maaaring magdulot ng karagdagang pagpalago ng iyong puhunan.

- Do not touch your invested money until you are ready to retire.

  Higpitan ang sarili at huwag galawin ang mga salaping nakalagak hanggang handa ka nang magretiro.

KsK Commandment #7 - Assess risks and options: The higher the return, the higher the risk

All investment opportunities come with risks.

AS WE DISCUSSED previously, if you know how to use time and compound interest to your advantage, you don't need to put your money in risky investments.

In Chapter Three, I told you about the story of Mr. F & Mrs. G. I narrated how they lost more than PhP 2 Million when they decided to invest money in a business they were not even sure really existed. The mistake they committed was obviously a result of misplaced trust, lack of study and simple carelessness. They were lured by the high interest rate even if they knew that very few legal businesses could offer that kind of revenue. They focused their attention only on the promised rewards. They did not consider whether the person who made the promising offer really had the capacity to deliver on her promises. They assumed that the borrower was credit-worthy just because a trusted friend endorsed her.

We must always keep in mind the risks involved every time we enter into any transaction. Let us keep in mind that: *Walang siguradong negosyo*. Always remember: when you are offered the opportunity to invest in something, you are actually being asked by whoever made that offer to lend them your money.

All investment opportunities come with corresponding risks. We must carefully assess the risks. We need to ask ourselves if we can really afford to lose the money we are investing, just in case the investment turns sour.

Apart from understanding the risks in a given investment, you must also know your own risk profile. Your life stage, your age, your health condition and your own financial obligations are very relevant in assessing what risks are appropriate for you. The extent and timing of the risks you take must be consistent with your financial goals.

Successful investing requires that the investor's risk profile matches with the type and extent of the attendant risks in a given investment.

Assess the risks involved every time you have to make choices and decisions in your journey to financial freedom. Below is a list of inherent risks in investing:

- **Risk of non-payment**
  This has to do with the financial credibility and character of the person or institution borrowing or making the investment offer. *Mayroon ba silang history of non-payment?*

- **Risk of liquidity**
  What is the liquidity of the investment or asset you are buying or lending money to? How fast can you turn it into cash when you need to? What is your real need for the money you are investing? How long can you do without it? *Mayroon ka bang ibang pagkukuhanan ng cash kung sakaling mangailangan kang bigla?*

- **Risk of inflation**
  Money is an ever-declining value. Your asset or investment must grow beyond the inflation rate. *Ang kikitain mo ba sa investment na ito ay mas mataas sa rate of inflation?*

- **Risk of new taxes**
  The government may decide any time to impose a new tax. This is always possible and you have to prepare for it. What will happen to this investment if there is a change in taxation?

- **Regulatory risks**
  This is related to anything the government decides to do that may change the rules of the game. Most of the time,

this is unlikely. However, you should still try to understand its effect on the profitability of your investment if the government changes its rules.

- **Business risks**

  This has to do with market, production and finance risks relevant to how the business produces the product or service and how it is financed and delivered to the consumers. How stable is this business you are investing in? *Baka naman ang negosyong ito ay "fad" lamang. Uso lang na di naman tatagal. Gaano karami ang mga kumpanyang makakalaban mo? Gaano sila katatag?*

  Is there sufficient history of profitable operations? Or is this just a start-up business? Does the business have sufficient sources of financing for equity or working capital? *Suportado ba ng mga bangko ang negosyong ito? Sino ang mga nagpapautang sa negosyong ito?*

- **Fraud risks**

  This has to do with the integrity of the business process and how it is documented. Is the investment documentation complete and legally binding? Do you fully understand the business logic, i.e., are there enough margins in the product price to provide for all overhead and marketing expenses? Do you fully understand the business process, i.e., how the products are produced, sold, collected and accounted for?

- **Foreign exchange risk**

  This has to do with devaluation or revaluation of the peso. Will your investment improve or suffer if there is devaluation or revaluation? You need to understand this factor as it relates to the long-term valuation of your investment.

Understanding a Loan versus an Investment

Ask yourself: Am I lending my money or am I investing it? A lender requires the payment of interest and the return of the principal amount he lent out.

What is a LOAN?

Usually a borrower must give a collateral to the lender to secure the loan. Banks normally ask for cash or real estate collateral equal to 170% of the loan amount. Understand that a responsible bank does not give out loans just because there is adequate collateral.

Ang bangko ay nagpapa-utang dahil may nakikita silang lehitimong pagkukuhanan ng pang-bayad.

The only correct basis for the granting of loans is the ability of the borrower to prove that he will use the proceeds of the loan in an activity that will produce sufficient income to repay the loan.

To make sure that he gets back his money, a lender gives out loans only when:

- The borrower has more than enough sustainable income to pay for the loan plus interest; and/or,

- The lender really does not mind foreclosing on or taking over the collateral. *Talagang gusto ng nagpapautang na mapasakanya ang kolateral sa halaga ng kanyang pautang.*

If you want to be a successful lender, you should follow this practice. Never, never lend money just because there is good collateral, unless you want that collateral at the price of the loan you gave. Just make sure that you know that the price of that collateral can go down in value with time. *Maaaring bumaba ang halaga ng kolateral pagdaan ng panahon.*

What is an INVESTMENT?

Investing in a company effectively makes you a partner in the business. The money that you put in as investment or capital is called equity. This equity, whatever the amount, will be at full risk. You make money when the business makes money and you lose money when the business loses money. In investing, usually the institution/s offering such investment products do not guarantee earnings and return of the principal. They make best estimates based on extensive financial and operational studies conducted by reputable professionals.

Walang kasiguraduhan na ipinapangako ang isang kumpanya kapag ikaw ay inaalok na sumali sa kanilang negosyo bilang isang investor.

Usually, the value of your investments rises or falls, depending on the profitability of the business you invested in. However, there is an added risk in the stock market. The values of the best stocks in the market fluctuate. These could go up or down, sometimes based on rumors, sometimes based on facts. The selling price (real value) of a stock is ultimately dependent on the investing public.

On the other hand, when you invest in shares of stocks that are not listed in the stock market, the ability to take out your money is somewhat limited. There is no established way to withdraw your investment when you so need. Generally, you become dependent on the controlling shareholder and/or the management if you want to sell your investment.

Each private investment transaction is unique. Each one is different from the other. If you invest in a private offering, you must make sure that you understand:

🔅 How income is being produced

🔅 Who else is investing and

🔅 Most importantly, how you can or how you will get back your investment when you want your money back

Beware of Scams

Why do people get victimized by scams? Very often, people fall victim to scams simply because they are not really clear on what they want. Again, as we discussed in Chapter Three, they just have this general idea of earning extra money.

There are two basic rules to follow before you take out money from your pocket to buy a product and/or to invest.

> 💡 The first consideration is personal.
>
> 💡 The second consideration is whether or not the offering and the company that is making the offer is legitimate and credit worthy. Generally, scams offer very attractive and unbelievably high returns. As they say, your most likely reaction is "it is too good to be true". If that is so, then most likely, IT IS REALLY TOO GOOD TO BE TRUE. *Talagang malamang hindi totoo ang pangakong pinansyal.*

Personal considerations

When offered to join a network, ask yourself the following questions:

> 💡 What is my interest in joining this network?
>
> 💡 Will I buy the product because I need it?
>
> 💡 Will I buy it because it is only available from this network?
>
> 💡 Will I buy it because I am getting a very good discount?

If your answers are NO to the above, or if it is clear that your interest is not to buy but rather to make extra income, ask these questions further:

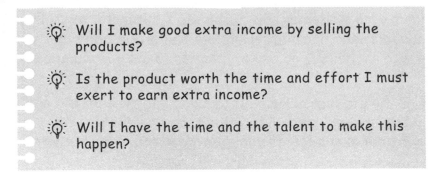

> :🔆: Will I make good extra income by selling the products?
>
> :🔆: Is the product worth the time and effort I must exert to earn extra income?
>
> :🔆: Will I have the time and the talent to make this happen?

If the answers are again NO, then walk away from the offer and save yourself time and money.

It is very important to be clear and sure about your personal purpose in putting your money in an offering. Do not put out money unless you are clear on what PERSONAL OBJECTIVES OR BENEFITS you stand to make out of the transaction. You have to be very clear about what you can expect to receive and, more importantly, WHAT YOU HAVE TO PERSONALLY INVEST IN TERMS OF MONEY, TIME AND TALENT.

However, if your answers are YES and you want the extra income because it is very attractive, study the system further. Pursue the specific objective of finding out whether the offering is, in fact, based on sound business operations, whether or not it is legal and whether, in fact, the company and the agent making the offer are duly licensed.

If you are not careful, you might become a victim of unscrupulous individuals and companies. They set up businesses for the sole purpose of deceiving investors with the promise of high returns. For example, many people have fallen into the trap of investing their hard-earned money in pyramiding schemes disguised as legitimate multi-level network marketing firms. Here are some questions that you need to ask before you make a decision to put out your money.

- Is the product something that will benefit a person and is legitimately priced? *Talaga bang bibilhin mo yung produkto sapagkat kailangan mo at tama ang presyo?*

- Is there a transaction? Is there a document or contract outlining the details of the transaction that you can understand? *Naiintindihan mo ba ang kasulatan at detalye ng inyong kontrata?*

- Is there an actual cash outlay? Do you need to pay a certain amount before you can be a party to the transaction? *Maglalabas ka ba ng pera para sumali sa network o para bilhin ang produkto?*

- Is the money being "pooled"? When the money goes into the business, is it kept in the business for the business? *Importante na hindi lumalabas ang pera para gamitin sa ibang layunin.*

- Is a third party managing the pool of money? *Yun bang mga perang nilalagak ng mga miyembro ay pinagsasama-sama at may namamahala na mapagkakatiwalaan upang ito ay lumago?*

• Is there a promised reward or profit? *Mayroon bang pinangako na kita kapag sumali ka sa network?*

If the answers to all of the questions above are YES, then the product being offered is an investment product or a security. Investment products or securities fall under the jurisdiction of the Securities and Exchange Commission (SEC).

The Securities and Exchange Commission

Do not be content with the Articles of Incorporation issued by SEC, which most investment proponents present as proof of their legitimacy. These Articles of Incorporation are just like the birth certificate of a person. *Ito ay pagpapatunay lamang na ang kumpanya ay "pinanganak" or binigyang buhay na ng SEC. Pero hindi ito sapat na karapatan para ang kumpanya ay pumasok sa pagbebenta ng investment products or securities.*

A legitimate company still has to:

Register its investment products with the SEC

Secure a specific license from SEC to sell them

Secure specific licenses from SEC for each of their agents to sell them

You should always ask for a copy of their product registration as well as the company's and the agent's license to sell them to the public.

157

A real lesson in investing

Ms. E is one of the many Filipinos in Hong Kong who were duped into investing their hard-earned money into Multitel, a pyramiding scheme. Ms. E narrated how frustrated she is with the government for allowing her, and many others, to become victims of the scam.

She blamed the government because she perceived that Multitel had its full backing and support. She based this perception on these factors: When she was encouraged to invest in the company she was shown Multitel's incorporation papers, duly approved by the Securities and Exchange Commission; and she was also shown an advertisement that came out in some publications announcing the launch of Multitel, with two senators gracing the event.

To Ms. E, the SEC incorporation papers and the advertisement with the pictures of the two senators were enough proof of Multitel's legitimacy. After seeing these, she did not think twice about investing her savings of Php 300,000 in the company. It was too late when she realized that she was the victim of a scam.

Ms. E had been working in Hong Kong for the last 10 years. The Php 300,000 she lost to Multitel was her life savings.

Her story should be a lesson to us that a company's incorporation papers are not sufficient proof of the legitimacy of its business. Neither are endorsements of government officials sufficient guarantee of an investment's potential. It is highly probable that those government officials were only invited to grace the event without knowing that the company is planning to get into something fishy.

Now Ms. E has learned that the best thing to do is to fully analyze and study a business or investment opportunity thoroughly before parting with her hard-earned money.

Investment Scams

Appendix A is a primer on scams provided by the SEC.

In response, however, to the many calls we have been receiving in our "Philippines Tonight" radio program, let me just discuss one of the most common type of scams promoted in the Philippines, Hong Kong, Singapore and the Middle East. This has to do with a multi-level pyramid scheme.

This system is promoted as a marketing system in support of selling personal products such as shoes, cosmetics, wardrobe and similar items. It entices members by proposing a joining fee, which entitles the new member to all the benefits of the system, namely discounts or gift certificates to redeem highly-priced products. More importantly, high "investment returns" in the form of fees and commissions are offered when the member is able to recruit new members into the organization.

If we ask the following questions to check the legitimacy of the scheme, we will understand what is wrong or right with it:

• Is there a real exchange of goods? Are the prices of the products about the same as the prices of the same products in retail or department stores?

- Are people really interested to buy the products in their product catalogues?

- Can the products of the type and size you want really be immediately delivered to the buyers of the products?

- Are the fees and commissions offered to members actually drawn from the joining fees and not from the sale of the products?

- Is the Offering registered with the SEC?

- Is the company and are its agents licensed to sell the system?

If you answer NO to the foregoing, ask the following questions:

- Is there a joining fee?

- Are the products or discounts you are entitled to, after joining, worth less than the amount of joining fee you pay?

- Are you really busy recruiting "down lines" more than selling the product so you can make money? In effect, are your fees and commissions coming from the joining fees of the new members?

If you answered YES this time, the scheme, from all indications, is a scam. It is classic pyramiding. Recruits are enticed to join because of the promised high return from their joining fee. The only way to make money is to recruit new members! This type of marketing system is highly suspect and most likely illegal.

These schemes, like the notorious Multitel, are generally short-lived. There are no real business transactions that can sustain the business. Sooner or later, the new members will run out of recruits. They end up losing their joining fees and starting capital and the pyramid crumbles. Unfortunately, it is the latecomers that get hurt! The organizers and the early birds get away with lots and lots of money!

You can do it. *Kaya mo 'to!*

- There are risks in every money transaction. Understand the details of every transaction and identify what kind of financial risks are applicable.

    Alamin ang puno't dulo ng bawat transaksyon. Intindihin kung anu-anong uri ng panganib ang maaaring magpawalang halaga ng iyong "investment".

- There is a technical difference between a loan and an investment. In a loan, your principal and interest are required to be paid back. In an investment, you become a partner in the business and you get your money back only if the business makes money.

    Alamin ang pagkakaiba ng nagpapautang sa "investment" o pamumuhunan. Ang pautang ay nangangailangan ng patubo at pagbalik ng prinsipal sa nagpautang. Kadalasan, ang umuutang ay hinihingan ng bagay na panggarantiya sa pagbayad ng inutang. Kapag ikaw naman ay nag-invest o namuhunan, ikaw ay nagiging kapartner sa negosyo. Sa ganitong katayuan, ang kita ng iyong puhunan ay nakasalalay sa kikitain ng negosyong nilagakan ng iyong salapi.

- Learn to identify scams.

    Suriin at intindihin ang mga puntos na maaaring maging mga senyas na ang inaalok sa iyong transaksiyon ay isang tinatawag na "scam" o panloloko lamang.

CHAPTER 18

KsK Commandment # 8 - Make money work for you: the power of leverage.

A good debt is an instrument for growth.

LEVERAGE, in finance, is borrowing. Debt is an instrument for growth but it has to be well planned and well studied. It makes your money and money that does not belong to you work for you.

It is not wrong to borrow money. It only becomes wrong when the borrowed money is not able to generate income to pay for the loan. But properly arranged, it could be what is called a "good debt".

Let us take a look at buying a house. Let us suppose that you have decided to buy a low-cost house. It is offered to you for PhP 500,000 with 20% down (PhP 100,000) and 15 years to pay at 6% per year interest. Monthly amortization is PhP 3,375. Let us also suppose that you have savings of PhP 500,000 cash in small denomination long term T-bonds earning 10% per year. Your household income is PhP 25,000 per month. You believe you can afford the monthly amortization. Your wife, like so many others, does not like to be in debt. Would you buy the house for cash or terms as offered?

Below is a comparison of the two options you have. It shows that this is an opportunity to enter into good debt. As illustrated below, by continuing to invest your available PhP 400,000 (after payment of the down payment) in the 10% T-bonds, you will be able to pay all your amortization from your existing savings of PhP 400,000 that earn 10% with more than PhP 900 per month left to reinvest. And reinvesting this amount again at 10% will give you an additional future savings of PhP 382,556 in 15 years.

POWER OF LEVERAGE: GOOD DEBT vs. BAD DEBT
PESOS (PhP)
BUYING A HOUSE:
Two Options:
1. Acquire it Cash
2. Acquire it through a loan

	OPTION 1	OPTION 2
Cash on Hand	500,000	500,000
Cost of House	500,000	500,000
Mode of Acquisition	Cash-Full Payment	15 yr loan; 20%down payment at 6%/yr
Downpayment	0	100,000
Cash Available for Other Investments	0	400,000
Monthly Amorization	0	3,375
Property value after 15 yrs growing at 5% per year	1,039,464	1,039,464
Total amortization paid out over 15 years	0	607,500
Total amount paid over 15 years	500,000	707,500
Monthly collection if Php 400,000 is placed at 10% p. a. over 15 years		4,298
Available cash after monthly loan payment		923
Value of Php 923 if invested monthly at rate of 10% p. a. over 15 years		382,556
TOTAL VALUE OF HOUSE AFTER 15 YEARS	1,039,464	1,422,020
GAIN DUE TO GOOD DEBT		`**382,556**`

Ang pinakapunto ng paggamit ng "leverage" o pingga ay yung paggamit ng utang na magdudulot ng karagdagang kita na higit pa sa obligasyong pinansyal na iyong aakuin sa iyong utang. Kapag ito ay iyong magagawa, mapapalago ng "leverage" ang iyong puhunan taun-taon. Sa ganitong paraan, hindi imposibleng dumoble o magtriple o higit pa doon ang iyong puhunan.

Because leverage is borrowing, I believe all of you are somehow availing of the power of leverage. Leverage allows you to get money now against the money you expect to earn in the future. It allows you to acquire something today with money you will still earn in the future. We see this every day that you use your credit card to buy all kinds of products or services. In fact, I believe, most people have abused this tool.

Leverage is a two-edged sword. Properly used, it delivers life-long advantages. Improperly used, it can drag you to the poor house. This is the case with most employees who are neck-deep in credit card debt. Without financial discipline, it is so easy for income earners today to get into the credit card trap.

Credit cards are practically shoved down your throats by companies who send them to you for free. They are even offered with credit limits you don't even ask for. And the temptation to use them is almost irresistible, especially when you are in a mall during the so-called "midnight sale".

The greatest risk in borrowing is the need for you to ensure yourself of a steady stream of income that should be large enough to pay for the principal and interest that is billed to you with such efficient regularity. It is noteworthy that in many cases, interest rate floats or changes periodically. This means that your interest rate may change every year and such eventuality should be prepared for.

Ang interes ay maaaring mag-iba buwan-buwan o taun-taon depende sa kasunduan. Kailangan maintindihan ito upang makapaghanda ng sapat na pambayad.

In the unforeseen event that you lose your source of income, you could lose all your physical assets and worse, your reputation. Lose this and you lose your capacity to rebuild again. The danger of leverage cannot be over-emphasized.

Ang pangungutang ay maaring makabuti o makasama. Alamin maigi kung mayroon pagkukunan ng pambayad sa utang sa buong panahon na nakatakdang bayaran. Marami sa atin ay pumapasok sa utang dahil mayroon nang pang "down payment" ngunit wala namang siguradong kita na mapapagkunan ng pambayad ng "amortization" buwan-buwan o taun-taon. Kadalasan, nareremata lamang ang bahay o kung anumang ari-arian na nabili sa installment.

The irony of it all is that you could get into debt trouble by being a good debtor. If you are so religious in your payment of your credit card obligations, you will find that you will become a much sought after client of credit card companies. You will get so many credit card offers that unless you really have the will to resist, you will end up availing of more credit than you need. So many have fallen into this trap and are practically working just to pay their debts.

*Kapag marunong kang magbayad
ng utang, liligawan ka naman ng
mga kumpanya ng Credit Card
upang alukin ka nang higit pa sa
kailangan mo. Kinakailangan na
mag-ingat ka sa tuksong ito.*

Here are some guidelines that might help you avoid leverage
or debt problems:

- As much as possible pay in cash. Borrow only if your cash
  will earn higher than the cost of your borrowing.

- Under present economic conditions, do not assume that
  you will always be in your present employment. Be
  conservative and do not assume that your current active
  income will continue to increase. This will help you in
  evaluating whether you should borrow or not.

- Make sure you know how much of your present income is
  being used to service your debts. If you are allocating too
  much of your income to pay your debt, you are over-
  leveraged.

- Never borrow for wants. Borrow only for needs, and only if
  you have to.

Some of the situations where leverage may be prudently used are as follows:

- Buying a home
- Improving a home
- Starting a business
- Cost of major and necessary medical treatment
- Paying for tuition
- Buying a car or any big ticket item that will be used to generate self-liquidating income

Another form of leverage is people leverage. For example you avail of leverage when you join a professional network of marketers and take advantage of generating extra income through legitimate uni-level, multi-level or direct selling companies. If you manage your time and your organization properly, you can develop "down lines" that can give you commission income without you having to spend time selling. This is people leverage as opposed to financial leverage in securing good debt.

Sa lipunang Pilipino, "leverage" o pingga ay bayanihan. Ito ay samahang nagpapagaan ng mga gawain. Sa mga bagay pinansyal, ang pangkaraniwang paggamit ng pingga o panikwas ay nakikita sa ating gawiin na tinatawag na paluwagan.

You can do it. *Kaya mo 'to!*

- Leverage is borrowing money for a good purpose provided the money received from the loan is able to generate income to pay for the loan.

  Ang paggamit ng pingga sa buhay pinansyal ay ang pag-utang. Ang tamang pag-utang ay makapagdudulot ng malaking tubo o pakinabang. Ito ay mangyayari lamang kung ang inutang ay nakalilikha ng kita na sapat o higit sa pambayad ng interes at ng prinsipal na inutang.

- Understand the various ways of using leverage in a helpful way.

  Pag-aralan at intindihin ang mga mabuting paraan sa paggamit ng "leverage".

CHAPTER 19

KsK Commandment # 9 - Invest and diversify

You should spread the risks.

BECAUSE there is always some risk involved in every business or investment opportunity, you must never place all your eggs in just one basket.   Prudence demands that, whenever possible, you should spread the risks.   Remember there is no sure business.   So many things beyond your control can go wrong. Make sure that the investments you make are properly matched with controlled risks.

Remember these commandments when you are in the process of evaluating business and investment opportunities. Investing though is not simply looking for opportunities and high returns.   Investing like anything else must always match a specific purpose.

When you buy a washing machine, for example, you buy it because you need or want one. So also when you invest, you must know exactly why you are doing it. Your expectation of the investment returns should be very clear as to amount and time of income.

But investing is not only about the amount of income. You must also understand what the return on investment (ROI) or yield *(kita ng iyong puhunan)* is.

In finance, this is the percentage return that an investment delivers based on the amount of principal capital you put in. The more complete way to understand investing is to view it like a triangle:

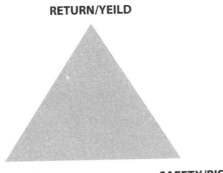

Every investment you make must be evaluated in terms of:

- Return: what is my yield *(kita sa puhunan)* or return on this investment? Is it higher than inflation?

- Liquidity: how long will my money be tied up? May I withdraw anytime and convert it back to cash?

- Safety of capital: how safe is this investment or what are the risks of losing my capital? *Ano ang posibilidad na mabawasan o maubos ang puhunan ko?*

Then you need to ask yourself:

- Why am I interested in this investment? What is the specific goal that this investment will achieve?

- Will it bring me closer to my target net worth? If so, how much closer? Two years? Five years?

- How much of my investible funds or my present net worth am I putting at risk in this investment?

- Do I have to decide now? Will this investment opportunity continue to be available tomorrow, next week, next month, next year? (Maybe you can sleep on it first)

- Is the financial return or income I stand to gain commensurate to the risk I am taking? Sometimes it is not only money you are putting at risk. It may also include family relations, reputation, your job security and other personal, professional relationships.

In this section, I will discuss some investment and business opportunities that I highly recommend especially for those who are still in the Start-up Phase of their financial life. These are:

- Government securities and other short-term investments

- Investment and Business Opportunities

What are government securities (GS) and other short-term investments?

Government securities are certificates of indebtedness issued by the national government with a promised yield that is backed up fully by the state. GS are classified as the safest investment instrument because it is guaranteed by the national government. It is also the most liquid as you can sell it at any time and there are always buyers.

There are several types of GS. The following are guaranteed by the national government:

- Treasury Bills (including Small Denominated T-Bills)

- Treasury Bonds (including Small Denominated T-Bonds)

- Progress Bonds (to generate funds for privatization)

- Home Guaranty Corp. (HGC) Bonds (full government guaranty)

- ERAP Bonds (full government guaranty)

- Agrarian Reform Bonds (full government guaranty)

T-bills are certificates of indebtedness that mature within one year or less. T-bills come in the following tenures: 91-day, 182-day, and 364-day.

T-Bonds, on the other hand, are certificates of indebtedness that mature beyond one year. T-Bonds come in the following tenures: 2, 5, 7, 10, 15, 20 and 25 years. There are different kinds of T-Bonds: Retail Treasury Bonds targeted for the retail market; Dollar denominated T-Bonds; Progress Bonds, among others. During the Erap administration, the government introduced the Small Investors Program (SIP), which reduced the minimum amounts for T-Bills and Bonds to as low as PhP 5,000 per investor. This gave rise to what is known as the Small Denominated T-Bills, T-Bonds and T-Notes.

If you want to invest in GS you can go to any of the 47 GS eligible dealers accredited by the Bureau of Treasury. These are mostly banks. The rates offered for these securities, once they are already in the secondary market, may vary slightly from dealer to dealer so I advice you to shop around. Call up several dealers, compare their rates and choose the one offering the best return for your money. You should also do the same when you sell them. Banks will always buy back your GS whenever you need to sell them. You must also remember that there is a 20% tax on income on GS.

If you are currently based abroad and would like to invest in GS, you can go to a branch of a Philippine bank there and purchase GS. The next time you return to the Philippines for a vacation, you may also enter into an agreement with your local bank granting them authority to auto-debit or auto-credit your savings account and invest it in GS.

Apart from GS, you may also invest in other short-term instruments like short-term commercial papers issued by Rated A companies like Ayala Corp., San Miguel Corporation, Globe Telecom, Unilever, PLDT, Smart, Procter & Gamble, among other companies.

For those beyond Start-up Phase, you have more options to invest your money. You can consider income-earning real estate, shares of stock of listed companies, contributions to financially sound cooperatives, foreign exchange denominated investment instruments, direct investments in ongoing businesses and many more. The general principle though is that the older you get, the less risks you should take.

You may also invest in Mutual Funds and Unit Investment Trust Funds (UITF) being offered by financial institutions. These funds are managed by professional fund managers and invested in attractive investments. You may inquire from different financial institutions about their mutual fund and UITF products to find what would suit your needs best.

No single investment will be able to meet ALL your financial objectives.

Investment and Business Opportunities

You are now aware of the risks involved in every investment and business opportunity and the many scams that you should avoid at all cost. You can now look into investment and business opportunities that will serve as your vehicle in your journey to financial freedom.

Kailangan mo nang alamin kung saan mo ilalagak ang iyong pinaghirapang kita upang lumago.

In my radio program, callers often ask me about business decisions they've made. Most of the time, they enter into

176

businesses without first fully studying the consequences of their decision. I have noticed too that they assume that they should go into a business that they can do on their own with whatever limited capital they have. Often it is also a business that is centered within their neighborhood or community.

Mas malimit, ang negosyo na gustong pasukan ng nakararami ay nasa kanilang sariling lokal, distrito, pamayanan o komunidad.

Except for a really entrepreneurial minority, most will go into businesses that are easy to enter. Some of these businesses are grocery or sari-sari stores, FX taxi business, tricycle business. For the majority who are not truly prepared, their attempt to go into business, more likely, will fail. To begin with, they enter businesses that are very often already very crowded. They end up going after small markets that cannot sustain too many sellers such as hot pandesal, sago drinks and fish balls.

Marami ay napapagaya lang sa mga umuusbong na negosyo at kahit kulang sa pagsusuri ay sumasabak na. Kadalasan dahil sa maling payo ng kaibigan o kamag-anak.

There are a few though who create their own opportunity using their own talent and personal resources.

Here's an example:

Cell phone repair has become quite popular in recent years because of the rising number of cell phone users. Most of those who want to get into the business think of setting up cell phone repair outlets. The owner of CellFix, however, took a different path. A communications engineer, he decided to offer a three-day course on cell phone repair instead of just setting up a repair shop. He charges his students PhP 10,000.00 for the course and a complete set of equipment, plus the right to open their own CellFix outlet. In addition to generating income from cell phone repairs, he is making money in training and sale of tools and equipment for repairing cell phones.

FRANCHISES

If you do not have any special skill like the owner of CellFix, I advise you to buy a franchise instead. There are now a lot of companies offering franchising opportunities. The advantage of getting a franchise is you minimize the risks involved in doing business. All production risks have already been defined and studied. All you need is to have the right motivation and training. There is no need for you to re-invent the wheel.

Getting a franchise is also one of the best ways to learn how to manage or run a particular business. When you buy a franchise you are also buying the opportunity to learn the whole business process, from sourcing of supplies to managing inventory, and handling people, among other things. The important thing is to LEARN.

Here are some things you need to consider when buying a franchise:

- Is the kind of business something you are really interested in? This is important because, contrary to common belief, when you get a franchise, you still have to be hands-on. The most successful franchises are still those run by the franchisees themselves.

- Relate it with what you are trying to achieve financially. Will getting into the business draw you closer to your financial goal? Is it in accordance with your personal financial plan?

- Assess the quality of the franchisor:

  - What is the track record of the company?

  - How many years has it been in business? Ideally, the franchisor should have been in business for at least three years.

- What are the terms of the franchise?

- What kind of training will they provide you?

- Will they give you financial support for supplies?

- What kind of support would they provide in terms of marketing and advertising?

- What do you get to own after terminating the franchise?

- Can you break the contract?

- How reasonable are the prices of the supplies you need to buy from them?

- Can you add other products or services?

- You also need to ensure that:

  - You will get a copy of the complete operations manual.

  - They show you their past financial statements.

  - They explain to you the business cycle and all the risks involved.

You can do it. *Kaya mo 'to!*

- Since there is no sure business, you must always spread your risks. As they say, "don't put your eggs in one basket."

  Maging maalam, maingat at masinop sa iyong pag-invest. Huwag ilagak lahat ng iyong puhunan sa isang "investment".

- Every investment you make must be evaluated in terms of return, liquidity and safety of capital.

  Timbangin ang mga sumusunod na aspeto sa bawat "investment" na papasukan: Ang laki ng kita, ang likwiditi o ang kadaliang ipagpalit sa "cash" ng puhunang nilagak, at ang laki o kawalan ng panganib na maaaring mawala ang iyong puhunan.

- Understand the various investment and business opportunities available. Franchising is one good option for most small businesses.

  Pag-aralan ang negosyong nakaprankisa. Ito ay maaaring magandang pang-umpisa ng mga baguhan sa pagnenegosyo o pangangalakal.

CHAPTER 20

KsK Commandment # 10 - Make use of the power of one: strength in numbers

Saving together provides better benefits.

LEARN AND SHARE with like-minded individuals.

A simple demonstration of this power of one is the ***paluwagan*** and the ***bayanihan*** concept, which we Filipinos have long been practicing. Here is another example.

There is strength in numbers

Ms. L is a 33-year-old domestic helper in Hong Kong. She was working there since 1994. During her first few years, she was not able to save. She was still single then and she felt that she owed it to herself to live it up somehow. After all, she had to endure a lot of difficulties in her work. She figured she should at least enjoy the fruits of her labor.

She regularly sent money to her family. But instead of saving what remained of her income, she spent it on clothes and other worthless items. She ended up spending all of her earnings. But after getting married in 1997, it dawned on her that she had to start saving so she could come home for good and start raising a family with her husband.

A nursing graduate, she wanted to practice her chosen profession in her hometown in Bicol. But before she could do that she knew that she needed to have sufficient savings to start a business that would provide her with additional income if and when she decided to work as a nurse back home.

Like most domestic helpers in Hong Kong, she earned HK$ 3,270 monthly. If she saved HK$500 monthly, it would take her some time to save enough money to start and operate a sizeable business that would provide her with a significant monthly income.

Instead of doing it alone, she encouraged six other domestic helpers from Bicol to start saving with her so they could save more in a shorter span of time. They knew that by having more money they could start a bigger business that would have a greater chance of succeeding than any business that anyone of them could set up on her own. They intended to use their joint savings to venture into a business in their hometown that one of them would have to directly manage.

About three years ago, each of them started saving HK$ 500 monthly. Today they have already accumulated more than half a million pesos that they have placed in time deposits and dollar savings accounts. Their savings continue to grow to this day as they consistently save more money monthly.

Whenever they have the opportunity, they attend seminars and workshops where they learn about investment and business opportunities they could get into. They are seriously studying and looking into profitable businesses where they could invest their savings. They are just waiting for the right time and opportunity. They hope that by next year one of them can come home for good to start and manage their dream business.

Their story is a good example of how working together, and in this case, saving together, can provide better benefits than doing it alone.

"The Power of One can lead to changes for the benefit of the many. These changes come from the many but only if the many can come together to form that which is invincible, the Power of One".

Anonymous

The case for would-be entrepreneurs

Statistics indicate that no more than 5 % of individuals who dare become entrepreneurs succeed. 95% end up losing their investments and end going back to employment (if they are lucky).

So what are the options for the 95%?

Most of these would-be entrepreneurs failed because:

- They lacked the business and management skills; and/or,

- They may have had enough in the beginning but miscalculated the working capital requirements and were thus unable to raise the correct financing when they needed it; and/or,

- They seriously mismanaged the operations of the business; and/or,

- They did not see the value of competent staff or consulting advisors in the areas of marketing, production, technology, legal aspects, personnel and most importantly leadership.

To this majority, I propose that you consider organizing into a cooperative or joining an existing legitimate cooperative. Individually, your capital to do business will definitely be small and inadequate. However, if you pool your resources in capital, talent and market reach, you will be able to form a formidable investment force that can provide you with:

- More high yield investment and business opportunities

- Greater probability for "no-capital-loss" of each member's contribution

- Greater ability to provide each member with the mechanism to convert his equity to cash in case of any urgent need

- Greater chances to earn higher and more consistent income because your collective investible funds will be substantial enough to warrant the attention of the most dependable and professional investment bankers

- Better access to the best professional management

- Assured financing for venture development and implementation

- Greater assurance for sustained success

For added information, Appendix B presents a primer on Cooperatives.

"Ang Kapangyarihan ng Isa ay makapagdudulot ng pagbabago sa kapakanan ng nakararami. Ang pagbabagong ito ay nagmumula rin sa nakararami kung ang nakararami ay magkakaisa upang makabuo ng isang puwersang hindi kayang gapiin, ang Kapangyarihan ng Isa."

You can do it. *Kaya mo 'to!*

- No more than 5% of individuals who dare to start up new business and become entrepreneurs actually succeed. 95% ends up losing their investments.

  Sa bawat isandaang tao na sumubok na magsariling negosyo, hindi lalampas sa lima ang nagtatagumpay at 95 ay nabibigo.

- Look into the option of banding together into cooperatives and the like.

  Isiping sumali sa mga kooperatiba o sa mga ibang uri ng mga samahan (tulad ng "savings & loan associations"). Ito ay malamang na makatutulong sa iyo sa pagpapalawak ng iyong kakayahan at sa pagbigay ng marami pang oportunidad sa pagpapalago ng iyong puhunan.

Your Way Ahead

CHAPTER 21

Determination, Discipline, Decisiveness

In good or bad times, never relent.

A STUDY of 300 world leaders including FD Roosevelt, Winston Churchill, Mother Teresa, etc. revealed that 25% had serious physical disabilities. An additional 50% had been abused as children or were raised in poverty. These leaders responded instead of reacted to what happened to them. They succeeded because they were determined, they were disciplined and they were decisive.

In the Philippines, we also have such leaders who responded to the challenges of their personal circumstances and came out winners. Ramon Magsaysay, an ordinary mechanic, went to become Secretary of Defense and eventually the seventh President of the Republic of the Philippines. Diosdado Macapagal, the poor boy from Lubao, became the ninth President of the Philippines. Jose Rizal, Gabriela Silang, Apolinario Mabini, the sublime paralytic, overcame financial, physical or political obstacles.

In recent business history, we see the successful trailblazers like, Henry Sy, John Gokongwei, Lucio Tan, Rolando Ortaleza of Splash, Carlos Chan of Oishi, Tony Tan Caktiong of Jollibee, Ben Chan of Bench. These are world-class Filipino entrepreneurs who are expanding their Filipino enterprises all over Asia and North America.

All these people reached their achievements because they were determined, disciplined and decisive. They all had vision and they never relented in good or in bad times.

These three D's are key to your success in reaching your financial independence. For purposes of this book, I define the three D's as follows:

- Determination is having the will and the persistence to do what you want to do.

  Kahit papaano, makukuha mo ang nasa isip mong gagawin.

- Discipline is the practice of regularly following certain methods and procedures to ensure success in your objective. Avoid short cuts, which are more and more getting to be the habit of most Filipinos. This is a bad habit brought about by too much rationalization. To get used to short cuts is to break down discipline.

Araw-araw, minu-minuto, gawin mo ang kailangang gawin upang mabihasa ka sa kinakailangan mong matutunan. Hindi ka dapat magsawa kahit paulit-ulit ito. Hindi mo dapat pahintulutan ang mag "short cut" sa trabaho. Ito ay magdudulot lang ng kabawasan sa antas ng produkto o serbisyo mo.

- Decisiveness is the willingness and the virtue to make decisions quickly, firmly and clearly.

Ang mga oportunidad ay hindi maghihintay sa iyo. Kailangan itong pag-aralan nang mabuti at desisyunan kapag alam mo na ang gusto mong gawin.

To emphasize the importance of the three D's, look at the true life stories in this book from:

- Mr. PJ who went from rags to riches, lost his riches and recovered them again.

- Mrs. AC who went into business without completely understanding the consequences.

- Mr. F & Mrs. G who readily believed their friend's friend.

- Mr. & Mrs. A who realized they spent too much on entertainment.

- Ms. S who from being "gastadora" is on the way to financial independence.

193

- Ms. L who understood the importance of pooling funds together to get a better deal.

- Ms. E who spent most of her life overseas to educate her siblings.

All of them have the common denominator. They were practicing the three D/s during the stage/s in their lives when they were successful.

But of the three D/s, what I want to emphasize is Discipline, which most Filipinos are sorely lacking in.

DISCIPLINE

Sa ikauunlad ng bayan, disiplina ang kailangan.

Maybe, some of you remember this "battle cry" of the government in the early 1970s. It was a very good reminder and it worked. However, after a few years, the very people who started it were the very ones who became undisciplined. Naturally, everybody seemed to relax and again do whatever he or she wanted without regard to the improvement of the country.

Filipinos in foreign countries are a more disciplined group than Filipinos in the Philippines. The reason is that Filipinos abroad mostly have to work harder and smarter since they are the minority. They also have to be perceived as better than the locals to be able to move up in their community.

This is for the readers who are OFWs or who travel abroad frequently. As you come home, perhaps, you can patiently continue to impart your experiences in the need for discipline to your families and friends. You become not only a financial provider but an educator as well.

Learning to say NO is part of discipline

I know that many of you have the same sentiment and are already sharing your wealth. However, I would also like to warn you of some possible regrettable situations.

If you are in business, it is wise that you keep certain aspects of your "genius" confidential to protect your own business. You must use your common sense in this respect.

Dapat gamitin mo ang iyong sentido kumon sa pag-alok ng iyong mga nalalaman.

If you are regularly sending money to your family and relatives back home, you must prepare a realistic budget for their needs. You must prepare this budget together with them so that you do not send them more or less than what they actually need. On the other hand, they should not be tempted to use the money for items not included in the budget. This will happen only if they know that you will not send any more than what you have agreed on.

Kinakailangang matatag ang inyong loob sa mga bagay na ganito. Kayo ang responsable sa inyong pag-iimpok. Nararapat lang na igalang ng inyong mga kamag-anak ang inyong pagmamalasakit sa kanila. Di dapat maging "martir". Bawat isa sa atin ay may angkop na pananagutan!

You can do it. *Kaya mo 'to!*

- Determination is having the will and the persistence to do what you want to do.

  Ang pagpupunyagi ay pagpapakita ng isang lakas na kaisipan at pagpupumilit na isagawa ang nais isagawa.

- Discipline is the practice of regularly following certain methods and procedures to ensure success in your objective.

- Decisivenes is the willingness and the virtue to make decisions quickly, firmly and clearly.

  Ang disiplina at ang kakayahang magpasya nang walang pag-aalinlangan hinggil sa mga bagay-bagay na may impluwensya sa iyong planong pinansyal ay ilan sa mga kinakailangan upang magtagumpay sa larangan ng "investments".

CHAPTER 22

Importance of Sharing

Sharing always brings back more blessings.

WHILE THIS IS a book on financial matters, I wish to dedicate this short chapter to emphasize the importance of sharing.

Life itself teaches us that sharing our blessings always brings back more blessings. This is especially true when we do not expect anything in return for the good that we do.

My entire life has been the result of good people sharing their blessings with me. As I mentioned at the beginning of this book, I was born four months before my father was killed leading the American forces into the University of Sto. Tomas. UST was then occupied by the Japanese as a prison war camp for captured Allied Forces.

I was able to study in one of the best schools and reach my present stature because of family, friends and benefactors who helped my family and me during our times of difficulties. There are so many of them that I dare not start to enumerate them for fear that I might miss out on some.

> But if life is really all about happiness, then we should learn this lesson by heart....

> "You have not lived a perfect day, even though you have earned your money, unless you have done something for someone who will never be able to repay you"

> *Ruth Smeltzer*

I want to emphasize that we must always share part of our wealth, whether it be in terms of money or talent or "genius".

Let me share Ms. E's story with you:

Ms. E is a 42-year old woman from San Fernando, Cebu. She is the eldest among six children. Her father is a farmer. Even as a young child, she already noticed that there was something wrong with the way her parents were raising them. Her parents never believed that they could have a better life. Fortunately for her and her siblings, she thought differently. She became determined early on to give her family a better life.

After finishing a two-year secretarial course, Ms. E worked for some companies in Cebu, which allowed her to send her siblings to school. However, the money she was earning was not enough. That was when she decided to go abroad and work as a domestic helper. She spent 11 years of her life abroad, enduring the loneliness brought by being away from her family, and the hardships that came with the nature of her work.

She endured it all because she knew that is the only way she could help her family. She decided to come home for good after 11 years, when her youngest sibling graduated from college. She said she has no regrets, despite all the hardships that she went through. For her, there is no greater joy than to see her family enjoy the fruits of her labor.

Ms. E's story teaches us that our quest to accumulate and build wealth will be meaningless if we cannot share it with others.

"We make a living by what we get; we make a life by what we give."

Duane Hulse

You can do it. *Kaya mo 'to!*

- Sharing our blessings will always brings back more blessings.

Huwag nating kalimutan na ang pamamahagi ng ating mga biyaya at kayamanan sa ating mga kasama at pamayanan ay magbabalik pa ng higit pang pagpapala at biyaya.

Starting
Your Journey

In sum here are the essential principles.

YOU ARE NOW set to start your journey to financial freedom or Kalayaan sa Kakapusan. It is my wish that you will have a safe and successful trip that will take you to your preferred destination on time. But before you go on that journey, let me share with you two letters.

These letters summarize all the rules and lessons that should guide you in living your financial life.

LETTER TO MY DAUGHTER LIA

The first is a letter of financial advice that I sent my daughter Lia shortly after she got married. Lia and Ferry started their married life in Europe in May 2002. I wrote this letter even before this book became an idea. In our family, we frequently discuss business matters so it was just natural for me to write the way I did. As I reviewed the letter, I realized that I had been expressing many of the ideas in my book even then.

Dearest Lia,

Here are my thoughts on the matter of personal financial planning which we have been discussing since your stint with me at TPG. Now that you and Ferry are independent and appear to be on your way towards family, professional and hopefully long-term financial success, I would like to share with you some of the essential principles, which I impart to the many budding entrepreneurs who consult with me on their personal finance strategies.

In the last year, I have seen a lot of successful entrepreneurs and independent contractors throw away their financial successes through reckless investments, or worse, ridiculous spending sprees. They all thought their cash flows would never end. They failed to prepare and plan for their future. They proved the adage: "The more you earn ... the more you spend".

As we all know, Li, SUCCESS IS THE MOST TEMPORARY THING IN THIS WORLD. Fortunately, FAILURE IS A NECESSARY INGREDIENT FOR SUCCESS. The key is to know how to learn from failures and have the discipline and determination to get up on your feet once again.

Since I help others so much, I would be remiss in my duty as a parent if I didn't try to guide you in your own financial concerns.

Underlying any financial plan is a set of premises why, to begin with, a financial plan is desirable among starting young couples. First is the acceptance of the reality that in our capitalistic world, the FIRST OBLIGATION of an individual (more so for married couples) is to build "wealth or capital" OVER TIME. The SECOND OBLIGATION is to PROTECT your ABILITY TO EARN. The THIRD is to ACHIEVE FINANCIAL INDEPENDENCE at each phase of your life, namely, start-up phase (20 through 35), build-up phase (35 through 45), fine-tuning phase (45 through 60) and finally, retirement phase (60 and above). The ages are estimates for you. In reality, one can be in any phase at any age depending on his financial achievement.

FINANCIAL INDEPENDENCE to me simply means a state of economic wealth where you have cash flow sufficient to meet your defined lifestyle needs WITHOUT having to work or put your own time in some economic activity to fund your daily and/or periodic needs. You are financially independent when you, OUT OF YOUR OWN CHOICE and not OUT OF NECESSITY, continue all the economic activity you engage in. In other words, you have enough cash flow (generated by your wealth) without having to work.

To achieve the above, you must first draw up your own FINANCIAL PROGRAM. This plan must DEFINE your TARGET level of PERSONAL NET WORTH when you are 35, 45 and 60. Your desired net worth on the other hand, must be arrived at based on your expected level of expenses consistent with the LIFESTYLE you choose. As a rule of thumb, ten percent of your net worth must be the amount of cash flow you will need to support your lifestyle ASSUMING you have no other source of income.

In your case, you and Ferry must make your worst projection on your current business or professional income from now through 35; from 35 through 45; and 45 through 60. If such level of income is insufficient to support your desired lifestyle, then the difference must be sourced from investments, other employment and/or new businesses you might have the opportunity to acquire or establish over the near or medium term.

I am simply bringing up the above points to remind you that the best and simplest tool in crafting your plan is to WORK BACKWARDS. You need to ESTABLISH YOUR FINANCIAL TARGETS and then DEVELOP SPECIFIC ACTION PLANS year-by-year.

Four very essential resources are available to you as you go about carrying out your business of building wealth towards long-term financial independence, namely: EMPLOYMENT, BUSINESS OPPORTUNITIES, COMPOUND INTEREST and TIME. Prudently combined, these four will guarantee your financial future.

The first requires personal competence. The second needs thorough and competent investment guidance. Availing of business opportunities entails real risks.

The last two have to do with LONG-TERM SAVINGS and WORKING KNOWLEDGE OF FINANCIAL INSTRUMENTS. In this regard, please know THAT BANKS, AS BANKS, DO NOT EXIST TO MAKE YOU WEALTHY. However, they can help, if you use them in the right way. Use Banks mainly for the CONVENIENCE OF TEMPORARY DEPOSITS and, if necessary, for BORROWING MONEY. But some banks and/ or their subsidiaries provide other collateral services such as trust funds and investment management, that can help you identify higher yielding opportunities.

Nevertheless, REAL CAPITAL GROWTH can never come from bank deposits.

I suggest you start off by defining the minimum level of lifestyle you would like to maintain and estimate how much monthly or yearly cash flow you will need for it.

Next, determine the level of sure cash flow both of you can depend on for the same period. In this regard, be clear as to what your primary income sources are. Know also if you have periodic secondary income sources (e.g. royalties, interest earnings, rental income, etc.). From this, you should be able to find out whether you have INVESTIBLE FUNDS, or money you can set aside for investments. The next challenge then is to determine what is the most prudent way you can allocate such investible funds. The best allocation (investment portfolio) must address the issues of risk, liquidity and long-term growth. NO ONE SINGLE INVESTMENT WILL BE ABLE TO MEET OR ANSWER ALL YOUR NEEDS AND/OR FINANCIAL OBJECTIVES.

Again, be sure to quantify your financial targets year-by-year or at least phase-by-phase. You are now in your start-up phase. During this period, your focus must be on YOUR NEEDS, NOT ON YOUR WANTS. All your disposable funds must be spent and invested wisely.

To summarize:

- Define your financial targets over the next ten years.
- Ferry should secure a term life insurance and a hospital income insurance plan, or if you want more coverage, a medical reimbursement insurance plan.
- Make your worst cash flow projections and determine your cash needs.
- Define how much money you can invest monthly or yearly.
- Allocate such "disposable" funds into sound short-term, medium-term and long-term investments.
- Once invested, LEAVE THEM ALONE. Let time and the power of compound interest work for you.
- Regularly AUGMENT your savings or investments to generate the growth in net worth you are targeting. This means that you should have the discipline to set aside a specific amount every month for placement in safe and sound investments.
- In all of the above, be guided by ONE PRINCIPLE. SPEND YOUR PRIMARY INCOME ONLY FOR YOUR NEEDS. FUND YOUR WANTS ONLY FROM SECONDARY OR OTHER SOURCES OF INCOME. As Robert Kiyosaki say: "Assets put money into your pocket... Liabilities take money out of your pocket." YOUR PRIMARY INCOME MUST NEVER BE SPENT ON THINGS THAT LOSE VALUE. (Exceptions to this rule might be cars and homes. These are used in the pursuit of livelihood and happiness, or could be legitimately classified as business expenses. Strictly speaking, they are not investments.)
- Finally, check out potential financial planners or advisors in your area. You should take advantage of their expertise. Believe me, it is worth the expense. In this regard, check out the following web sites: "ihatefinancialplanning.com" "ricedelman.com" or search out from "google.com" other financial planning sites.

I don't know your specific financial situation but I hope the above principles can help you and Ferry draw up your own financial plans. Just remember, in cash flow planning, PRESENT CASH IS MORE MEANINGFUL THAN FUTURE CASH.

I hope this letter will help you better prepare for your financial future. But in the end, what is important is your happiness with each other. Money should come second to spiritual commitment to one another. Money is just an idea as Ferry has proven. It's his talent that created his wealth. Your own talent can just as well create new opportunities for both of you.

This is it for now. Be assured, your mom and I keep you and Ferry in our prayers. Take good care Li. We love you very much.

Papa

LETTER TO MS. MARILOU SANTOS

My second letter is to Ms. Marilou Santos.
I have used her as an example throughout this book
and I know that she represents each and every
OFW to whom I have dedicated this book.
My letter to her summarizes the salient issues
discussed in this book.

Dear Marilou,

You have been my primary inspiration in writing this book. It is just proper that I end it with a letter to you.

Before anything else, on behalf of all Filipinos, I should express my sincere appreciation for all the support that you have given our country. At such great sacrifice, you left your family to be able to provide for them financially. At the same time, you reduced the unemployment rate in our country. While providing our economy with much needed dollars. You are truly a heroine!

I know that my advice in this book will surely help you if you follow them. If you are like Ms. S in Chapter 11 who is already practicing most of the principles I explained, this book is a good review. If this is the first time you are learning these principles, I am so glad that you have taken the first step.

Your primary reason for making your big sacrifice to leave your family is to earn a living to improve your financial status. We all know that it is quite important to you to build wealth or capital over time. You want to be able to reach a point when you will have enough cash flow to live the kind of life you want to live without having to work. That cash flow should come from passive income from your investments.

I am talking to you at the Start-up Stage of your life. This means that you earn only active income from employment and "sideline."

You can ensure that you successfully move on from the Start-up Stage of your life to Build-Up Stage, then to Asset Allocation Stage and finally to Retirement. Know your genius, know what you are really good at, and look for ways to use those gifts.

In your journey towards financial freedom, try to remember the KsK Ten Commandments that I explained:

#1: Pay yourself first. Always set aside 20% of your income for savings.

 # 2: Define your financial target at each Life Phase. Before anything else, know where you are financially today. Make your own Statement of Assets and Liabilities and your Personal Income and Expenses Statement. Keep track of the growth of your net worth. Review your SAL every year. Do not be discouraged by temporary setbacks. Make adjustments if you have to but never stop planning and assessing results.

#3: Don't spend on things that lose value. Especially, do not spend your active income on these things that you can do without, more so, if they are things that lose value.

#4: Protect your greatest income-generating asset: yourself.

#5: Grow with the economy and beat inflation. Look for savings instruments that give higher interest rates than inflation.

#6: Trust the power of compound interest. Time is of the essence. Once you put your savings in safe and long-term investments, leave it alone and let the power of compound interest work for you.

#7: Assess your options and study the risks: The higher the return, the higher the risk. Beware of Scams.

#8: Make money work for you. Work smarter not harder. By the way, there is such a thing as "good debt".

#9: Invest and diversify. Do not put all your investments in one basket.

#10: Use the power of one: strength in numbers. Join associations and learn from others.

Remember too to avoid the "tsaka na" habit or procrastination. Be guided by winners! As long as there is time, we can always move forward no matter how many failures we have had in the past. Do not be afraid to make mistakes. You can learn from them.

Always search for good advice from reputable and knowledgeable people.

Finally, your being an OFW is the biggest proof of your commitment to share yourself with others. However, I hope you will also be wise and protect yourself from the very people that you are helping. Make a budget, stick to it and don't be a martyr for your friends and relatives.

It would be even better if you will share what you have learned in this book with your relatives and friends. In this way, they will understand what you are doing and help you meet your financial objectives and in the process, perhaps, they will also grow financially.

Throughout this book, we have discussed all about how to achieve our financial well being, to accumulate wealth so that we can buy and enjoy the things money can buy. I hope though that in this process, you take special care not to lose the things and values that money can never buy.

Lahat ng ating napag-usapan ay upang magkaroon tayo
ng kasaganaang pinansyal. Napakasarap kung mayroon tayong
sapat na kayamanan upang makabili ng mga bagay
at ari-arian na nabibili. Huwag lang sana natin makalimutan
na pangalagaan nating huwag mawala sa atin ang mga bagay
na hindi nabibili.

Sumasaiyo,
FJC

Part 4

Appendices

A Primer on Scams

Source:
Philippine Securities and Exchange Commission (SEC)

How to spot a financial scam

In the past years, so many have lost a huge substantial amount of money to financial scams.

- Will you be the next victim?
- Do you know how to spot the clues?

It looks real

Scams that catch people often look realistic and are presented professionally. "Scamsters" often go to a lot trouble to:

- print attractive documents and set up a business-like website
- choose names that sound like reputable companies
- tell a persuasive story using the right jargon
- drop the names of people you know to build your trust

Five clues for spotting scams

1. Bigger and faster profits than real investments
Scams always offer a higher return than genuine investments. Some offer 20% a year, others go for 300% a year or even more. It's too good to be true. By comparison, Australian shares are some of the most successful investments, and their value has grown about 7-9% p.a. over the long term.

2. Less risk and less effort than real investments

Most scams say that financial success is easy and risk isn't a problem. But real wealth demands planning, hard work and guts. Even the best investors make mistakes and have to weather storms like market busts and economic recessions.

3. Something special that genuine investments don't offer

It could be a 'secret' offer, 'inside information' or 'new techniques'. There's always some feature to make you feel like you've got an edge over other people. But chances are it's a fairytale and it won't have a happy ending.

4. More urgent than the real thing

Every scam gets dressed up as an opportunity, so scamsters often say 'don't miss out' and 'act quickly' to make you hurry 'before it's too late'. They're really just trying to grab your money before you have a chance to check properly.

5. Offered by a stranger

Many scams come from overseas, through unsolicited email or surprise phone calls. Others get sold through 'wealth creation' seminars or on the grapevine. While the people can sound genuine, they rarely have any real credentials, such as an Australian Securities & Investment Commission (ASIC) license to give advice or sell financial products.

Ponzi schemes

One of the simplest, yet most effective scams perpetrated on unsuspecting investors for many years have been Ponzi schemes.
In these schemes the promoter promises investors a very high return on their investment and says it is secure.

Part of the money deposited by early investors is then used to pay their first dividend checks or interest. The victims are more than happy to get high dividends. These schemes only require a few people in their early stages to be successful.

The swindler continues paying them dividends for a couple of months until they are more comfortable with their investments, and decide to invest more.

They then begin to urge their friends and relatives to invest as well. Soon, there is a steady flow of funds into the scheme, and the number of investors grows.

If the swindler is disciplined about how much money is left in the account to pay "dividends", the scam can go on for many years. Theoretically, if the scheme continues to draw in new investors, it could go on indefinitely. In practice such schemes usually fall over because the promoter starts to spend the money too quickly, or the pool of investors starts to dry up.

Ponzi schemes

10% per month (120% per year) - Where do you get it?
A family friend was offered an "investment opportunity" returning 10% per month (120% per year) by someone in his church. Fortunately, the friend, who runs a successful mechanics' business, knows a bit about finance and refused.

Sadly, the person who tried to get him interested had already forked out PhP 100,000.

At 10% per month, the rate of return is so suspiciously high that this person will probably lose a great deal of money. It smells like a classic Ponzi scheme.

How Ponzi schemes operate

Let's call the victim Joe Blow. The crooks can pay Joe PhP 10,000 a month using his own money. They can pay Joe for seven months, if they steal only PhP 30,000 of his original PhP 100,000. That way they keep Joe happy and encourage him to recruit other people.

If Joe recruits Joanne Blow for the scheme at PhP 100,000, then the crooks can keep up his payments and give her some money as well. Joe and Joanne will be praising the scheme to the skies, and will be able to show all their friends their blossoming bank statements.

Maybe more people join. So long as the money keeps flowing into the scheme, payments can still come out. However, the burden of future payments also keeps growing. The scheme inevitably collapses once people stop joining.

A Ponzi scheme's cash flow month by month

Here's a worked example, assuming that the swindlers steal only 30% of everyone's money. (We have made them far too kind.)

Month	Investor	What investors pay in	What the crooks paid to investors	What the crooks pay themselves
Start	Joe Blow	PhP 100,000		PhP 30,000
Feb			PhP 10,000	
Mar	Joanne	PhP 100,000	PhP 10,000	PhP 30,000
April			PhP 20,000	
May	Bruce	PhP 100,000	PhP 20,000	PhP 30,000
June	Melanie	PhP 100,000	PhP 30,000	PhP 30,000
July	Raelene	PhP 100,000	PhP 40,000	PhP 30,000
Aug	David	PhP 100,000	PhP 50,000	PhP 30,000
Sept			PhP 60,000	
Oct			PhP 60,000	
Nov			PhP 60,000	
Dec			PhP 60,000	
The end		**PhP 600,000**	**PhP 420,000**	**PhP 180,000**

What's the bottom line?

The scheme runs out of money and collapses with nothing left to pay the investors by the end of December.

Joe, the first to join, got PhP 110,000 over the life of the scheme, which works out at 10% per year, not the 120% promised. The rest of the people all lost money.

David, the last one to join, suffered most. He put in PhP 100,000 and received only PhP 40,000 before the scheme collapsed, so he lost PhP 60,000. And the crooks? They got PhP 180,000 for nothing.

Danger awaits the inexperienced

Your church group may offer you many wonderful things, but it is not the place to hunt around for investments. Fraudsters and operators of unlawful investment schemes sometimes target church groups to find their victims.

Victims tend to be people who do not know much about investing, and so turn to others whom they know and trust. In some cases, church members have innocently encouraged each other to put money into fraudulent or unlawful schemes.

When the schemes collapse, then we see first hand the financial ruin, personal distress and breakdown of relationships among family, friends, neighbors and members of their church.

Pyramid schemes

In a nutshell, pyramid schemes promise to make you money. You pay the person who recruits you for the right to go out and recruit your new members to the scheme. In turn, they must pay you for their right to recruit their own new members.

Pyramid selling involves two payments:

● *What you pay*

There is an up-front participation payment that new members must pay to join the scheme. Generally this payment will entitle you to some goods or services. However, unlike a normal business deal, you do not get real value for money. The goods or services will be overpriced, and the only way you can recover your up front payment is by getting new recruits to pay you to join the scheme.

● *What gets paid to you*

You get a recruitment payment for getting other people to join. This is a substantial part of the reasón for joining.

Pyramid selling schemes have involved almost all the goods and services you could possibly imagine. Sometimes they have sold nothing more than the 'right' to recruit other people into the scheme.

How schemes build and then collapse

The scheme builds up layer upon layer of recruits, forming a pyramid. Every pyramid collapses.

People give up because they cannot sell enough to recover the money they originally paid to participate. They find it much harder than they think to sell overpriced goods or services, especially to friends and social contacts.

Schemes also inevitably run out of new recruits, although this may take some time to happen.

To show how this occurs, let's assume a tightly controlled scheme where everyone recruits only five people. The founder of the scheme sits at the top of the pyramid. The first five people pay the founder to be able to join.

These five people must now go out and find a second layer of five people each to pay them. By the time you get to the third layer, you need 126 people in the scheme. At the sixth layer, that number jumps to 15,626. Just two more layers, and you've outstripped the population of Canberra with 390,626. One more layer reaches 1.9 million people. If that's when the scheme falls over, then 1.5 million people lose their money.

Pyramid selling is illegal

Trade and Industry laws ban pyramid selling. If a pyramid scheme claims to sell financial products, then it's illegal under Securities & Exchange Commission Rules & Regulations. Financial products include shares, managed funds, superannuation, insurance, and credit.

Is it pyramid selling or marketing?

Sometimes it can be tricky telling the difference between a pyramid scheme and other schemes that may be perfectly legal. Essentially, it boils down to whether recruitment payments form a substantial part of the reason for you to join.

Here are two useful questions to help check if a scheme is legitimate.

● *Does your participation payment bear a reasonable relationship to the value of the goods or services that you get under the scheme?*

If not, it's probably a pyramid scheme.

Here's an example of how you might spot a pyramid scheme about selling car insurance.

You must pay PhP 1000 up front to participate. That entitles you to a discount of PhP 40 off your PhP 1,500 comprehensive car insurance.

You get promised PhP 100 for recruiting new people to the scheme.

Since the PhP 40 discount goes nowhere near recovering your PhP 1,000 up front payment, you only reason to join would be the recruitment payments. To come out ahead, you must recruit more than nine people into the scheme. This is an illegal pyramid scheme.

● *How much does the scheme emphasize the products compared with the recruitment payments?*

If recruitments payments get heavily emphasized, it's probably a pyramid scheme.

Here's an example of how you might spot a pyramid scheme about selling shares in a new internet business.

You must pay PhP 1000 up front to participate. That entitles you to 1,000 shares. The shares can only be sold back to the company or to other participants after 12 months. So you don't really have any idea what they may be worth.

You get promised PhP 100 in cash if you immediately recruit new people to the scheme.

You attend a promotional seminar for this scheme. The 90-minute seminar spends 70 minutes on how to recruit new investors and 20 minutes on the internet business. Since your shares are frozen for 12 months, and the scheme obviously pushes recruitment really hard, the recruitment payments form a substantial part of the reason for joining, making this another pyramid scheme.

Four safety checks to protect your money

● Take your time before investing your money.

● Research any investment. Only get involved if you understand the offer.

● Make sure you're comfortable with the risks, especially if you're borrowing to invest.

● Get information and advice from reputable people.

Avoid seminars that make these claims:

● 'You can become a millionaire in three years'

● 'Traditional investments are too slow and lack excitement'

● 'You can turn your financial dreams into reality'

● 'Amazing, fabulous, unbelievable strategies for building massive wealth'

Avoid sales people who:

● Pressure you into investing and/or borrowing money

● Promise you high returns with no explanation of risk

● Promise you access to 'secret' or 'exclusive' techniques for building wealth

● Lure you with free seminars only to hit you later with high fees

Don't get sucked in by:

● glossy brochures

● over-the-top testimonies from past customers

● pictures of people punching their hands in the air in triumph

● pictures of the promoter relaxing on his yacht

Cooperatives

What is a Cooperative? (General Concept of a Cooperative)

A cooperative is a duly registered association of persons, with a common bond of interest who have voluntarily joined together to achieve a lawful common social or economic and making equitable contributions to the capital required and accepting a fair share of the risks and benefits of the undertaking in accordance with universally acceptable cooperative principles.

Why form a Cooperative? (Objectives of a Cooperative)

The primary objective of every cooperative is to provide goods and services to its members and thus enable them to attain increased income and savings, investments, productivity and purchasing power and promote among them equitable distribution of net surplus through maximum utilization of economies of scale, cost-sharing and risk-sharing without, however, conducting the affairs of the cooperative for charitable purposes.

Purposes in Organizing a Cooperative

1. To encourage thrift and savings mobilization among the members;
2. To generate funds and extend credit to the members for productive and provident purposes;
3. To encourage among members systematic production and marketing
4. To provide goods and services and other requirements to the members.

5. To develop expertise and skills among its members.
6. To acquire lands and provide housing benefits for the members.
7. To insure against losses of the members.
8. To promote and advance the economic, social and educational state of the members;
9. To establish, own, lease or operates cooperative banks, cooperative wholesale and retail complexes, insurance and agricultural/industrial processing enterprises, and public markets.
10. To coordinate and facilitate the activities of cooperatives;
11. To undertake any and all other activities for the effective and efficient implementation of the provision RA 6938.

Cooperative Principles:

Every cooperative shall conduct its affairs in accordance with Filipino culture and experience and the universally accepted principles of cooperation such as:

1. *Open and Voluntary Membership*
Membership in a cooperative shall be voluntary and available to all individuals regardless of their social, political, racial or religious background or beliefs.

2. *Democratic Control*
Cooperatives are democratic organizations. Its affairs shall be administered by persons elected or appointed in a manner agreed upon by members.

3. *Member Economic Participation*
Members contribute equitable to and control the capital of their cooperative. At least part of that capital is usually common property of the cooperative. Members usually receive limited compensation, if any, on capital subscribed as a condition of membership. Members allocate surpluses for any or all of the following purposes:
- developing their cooperative, possibly by setting up reserves, part of which at least would be invisible
- benefiting members in proportion to their transactions with the cooperative
- supporting other activities as approved by the membership

4. *Autonomy and Independence*
Cooperatives are autonomous, self-help organizations controlled by its members. If they enter into agreements with other organizations (including government) or raise capital from external sources, they do so on terms that ensure democratic control by the members and maintain their cooperative independence.

5. *Education, Training and Information*
Cooperatives provide training and education for their members, elected representatives, managers and employees so they can contribute effectively to the development of their cooperatives. They inform the general public, particularly young people and opinion leaders about the nature and benefits of cooperation.

6. *Cooperation among Cooperatives*
Cooperatives serve their members most effectively and strengthen the cooperative movement by working together through local, national, regional, and international structures.

7. *Concern for Community*
Cooperatives work for the sustainable development of their communities through policies approved by their members.

Kinds of Cooperatives
Cooperatives may fall under any of the following types:
1. Credit Cooperative - promotes thrift and savings among its members and creates fund in order to grant loans for productive and provident purposes.
2. Consumer Cooperative - the primary purpose is to procure and distribute commodities to members and non-members.
3. Producers Cooperative - undertakes joint production whether agricultural or industrial.
4. Marketing Cooperative - engages in the supply of production inputs to members, markets their products.
5. Service Cooperative - engages in medical and dental care, hospitalization, transportation, insurance, housing, labor, electric light and power, communication and other services and
6. Multi-purpose Cooperative - combines two (2) or more of the business activities of these different types of cooperatives.

Categories of Cooperatives
In terms of membership, cooperatives shall be categorized into:
1. **PRIMARY** - the members of which are natural persons of legal age
2. **SECONDARY** - the member of which are primaries
3. **TERTIARY** - the members of which are secondaries upward to one (1) or more apex organizations.

In terms of territory, cooperatives shall be categorized according to areas of operations which may or may not coincide with the political subdivisions of the country.

Kinds of Membership
A **regular member** is entitled to all the rights and privileges of membership as stated in the Cooperative Code and the coops' by laws.

An **associate member** has no right to vote and be voted upon and is entitled only to such rights and privileges provided by the cooperative's by laws.

A cooperative organized by minors shall be considered a laboratory cooperative and must be affiliated with a registered cooperative.

General Steps in Forming a Cooperative
First: Get Organized. You must have at least 15 members to do that.
Second: Prepare a general statement called an economic survey. This statement will help you measure your cooperative's chances of success.
Third: Draft the cooperative's by-laws. The by-laws contain the rules and regulations governing the operation of the cooperative.
Fourth: Draft the articles of cooperation.
Fifth: Secure bond of your accountable officer(s), normally the treasurer or the treasurer and the manager.
Sixth: Register your cooperative with the Cooperative Development Authority (CDA).

Where to Register your Cooperative

The *Cooperative Development Authority (CDA)* is the only government agency mandated to register all types of cooperatives.

Its main office is located at 5th and 6th floors, Ben-Lor Building, 1184 Quezon Avenue, Quezon City.

General Requirements for Registering a Cooperative

Four (4) copies each of the economic Survey, By-Laws and Articles of Cooperation.

The Articles of Cooperation should be duly notarized and accompanied by the following:

- Bonds of the accountable officers.

- Sworn statement of the treasurer duly authorized showing that at least 25% of the authorized share capital has been subscribed of the total subscription has been paid.

  The paid up capital must not be less than PhP 2,000.00

It must be noted that no member may own more than 20% of the subscribed share capital; and each must not be less than PhP 1.00.

Acknowledgements

First and foremost, my deep appreciation to all who inspired me and started me off to research more and to share my knowledge on basic personal finance. These are the people from all walks of life who I work and have worked with, listened to my radio program, phoned in, wrote and emailed their questions. My very special thanks to the founders and marketers of Prozinergy and Future First whose personal successes encouraged me to spread the good news that financial independence is indeed within reach; to Sato Ridad, Yoly Miranda, Ruben Victorino and other senior officers who ably took over the presidency, finance and operations management of Professional Financial Plans that gave me the opportunity to start this advocacy.

To our able RMN co-anchor Buddy Oberas and the untiring technical and administrative staff, my sincerest thanks for ensuring the smooth operation of our radio program. Special acknowledgement also goes to Metro Broadcasting of Hong Kong, the home of the most supportive network to OFWs in Hong Kong.

For their generous, constructive and creative assistance, without which I could not have completed this book: Armand Q. Bengco, and Mary Elizabeth R. Bilgera of Colayco Foundation for Education, Inc., who helped flesh out my ideas and provided the back-room support; Joy M. Cabrillos who assisted in interviewing and writing the true-to-life stories in this book; Roger Laraya, a most competent investment advisor and colleague who helped me refine the Pilipino or Taglish summaries and certain key ideas; my daughter Ina and son-in-law Tonichi of INC Design Studio, Inc. who provided critical design, layout and printing consultancy that made my work so much more proficient and, I must admit, fun.

To my sisters, particularly Teresa, brothers, relatives and many friends and associates who generously contributed their ideas, wittingly or unwittingly, that helped and encouraged me to complete this book, my heartful thanks.

I cannot fully express my gratitude to the exceptional team of Michael Vincent Benares and Federico "Jun" Paragas (Tita Keri) of the Philippines Tonight Show radio program and the other officers and members of the forty thousand - strong Confederation of Overseas Workers, Hong Kong (COFW). They enabled us to launch the "Good Morning Pinoy Movement" for promoting personal financial literacy and provided the opportunity for the seminars in Hong Kong that further highlighted the urgency of coming out with this book.

My sincere appreciation to the major sponsors and resource persons of the seminars in Hong Kong: TPG Corp; First Metro Investment Corp. (FMIC); Cinco Management Holdings. Mobile Carwash, eBusiness Services, Inc. (eBIZ), Healthway, and Quam Limited.

I also would like to specifically acknowledge the invaluable assistance of Anthony F. Veloria who generously lent his time and talent in putting together the personal accounting guidelines discussed in this book. I owe much gratitude to many more supporters of our advocacy, such as Assistant

Finance Secretary Eleonor De La Cruz, Ms. Helena Valderrama, Chair of the Department of Accounting & Finance of the UP College of Business Administration and her key staff members who gave valuable insights and technical assistance in formulating and articulating specific financial literacy concepts embodied in this book; Neil Palabrica, Associate Publisher and Lyra Villafaña Editor-in-Chief of Entrepreneur Magazine for providing the various information on franchising and franchisors.

My gratitude for the support of the Cooperative Development Authority (CDA) particularly Administrator Dr. Virginia Teodisio, Division Chief Fe D. Caingles, and Atty. Danny Segobre Legal Head of CDA for providing both technical and substantive information on how cooperatives can help OFWs. To them I can only say maraming salamat po!

And finally, my never-ending gratitude and love to the five most important women in my life:

My mother, Clemencia J. Colayco who was mother and father to me almost from the day I was born. She was an excellent role model; one who rose from the burden of being a widowed teacher at the end of World War II and raised seven educated and professional children who were her pride and joy until she passed away 19 days short of 99.

My three daughters, Cessie, Ina (with husband Tonichi), and Lia (with husband Ferry), who are still in the Start-up phase of their financial lives. They have always interrogated me with the right questions to give me a better insight on the needs of those who want to start on their Financial Journey. Their continued belief in my capability sustains my eagerness to share whatever knowledge and experience I have accumulated.

And most of all, my most supportive wife, Mary Anne. She provided me with the inspiration and utmost zeal to launch this advocacy. She suffered so much stress attending to the details for this book to be published. It goes without saying that she served as the "devil's advocate" in threshing out the theories, premises and ideas posited in this work. In all, she was co-author, editor and manager who made this book a reality.

Reference & Research Sources

Edelman, Ric. Discover The Wealth Within You.
Harper Collins Publisher,
New York, 2002.

Edelman, Ric. The New Rules of Money.
Harper Collins Publishers, New
York, 1998.

Edelman, Ric. The Truth About Money.
Harper Colllins Publishers, New
York, 1996.

ICRA Bulletin. Money & Finance.
Tulika Print Communication Services, New
Delhi, 2003.

Kiyosaki, Robert. Rich Dad's Cashflow Quadrant.
Warner Books, New York,
2000.

Kiyosaki, Robert. Rich Dad, Poor Dad.
Tech Press, New York, 1998

Kobliner, Beth. Get A Financial Life.
Simon & Schuster New York: Fireside
Book, 1996.

Orman, Suze. The 9 Steps To Financial Freedom.
Crown Publishers, Inc., New
York, 1997.

Pollan, Stephen M. and Levine, Mark.
The Die Broke Complete Book of Money.
Harper Collins Publishers, Inc.,
New York, 2000.

Spurge, Lorraine. Money Clips.
Hyperion, 2000.

About the REGISTERED FINANCIAL PLANNER (RFP)

The RFP® designation is granted by the Registered Financial Planner Institute of United States to individuals who have committed to adhere to high standard of professional practice by voluntarily participating to the RFP certification process that includes continuing education, examination and experience requirements. The RFP® mark helps the client to recognize financial planners who are certification marks owned by Registered Financial Planner Institute of USA, which can help you identify financial planners who are dedicated to professional and ethical behavior when providing financial planning service.

The Registered Financial Planner Institute (RFPI) was formed in 1983 in Ohio, USA. It is an independent self-regulatory professional organization that provides education and membership in the financial planning industry. The RFP® was first used in commerce in 1983, filed in the United States Patent and Trademark office in 1987 and registered under the exclusive right in 1988.

The Institute is dedicated in promoting professionalism in financial planning and has become a prestigious global organization with members worldwide that includes USA, Canada, Hong Kong, China, India Singapore and now the Philippines.

LEARN MORE ABOUT:

Wealth Within Your Reach: Pera Mo, Palaguin Mo!
Making Your Money Work: Pera Mo, Palaguin Mo! 2
Pera Palaguin Workbook
Money For Kids: Pera Mo, Palaguin Mo!

Join the growing list of companies and participants of our seminars and workshops about the principles and concepts of the author and special guests who talk about managing your personal finances and various investment options.

Call Telephone Nos. 63-2-637-3741 and 631-4446 or
Text 63-917-8537333 or Fax 63-2-637-3731
www.colaycofoundation.com
email: info@colaycofoundation.com

- ✂ - -

Join:

JOIN KALAYAAN SA KAKAPUSAN SERVICE & MULTI-PURPOSE COOPERATIVE

Name: _____

Address: _____

Telephone Number: _____

E-mail: _____

Call Telephone Nos. 63-2-637-3741 and 631-4446 or
Text 63-917-8537333 or Fax 63-2-637-3731
www.kskcoop.com
email: kskcoop@colaycofoundation.com

- ✂ - -

REGISTER WITH US TO AVAIL OF SPECIAL OFFERS

Name: _____

Address: _____

Telephone Number: _____

E-mail: _____

Call Telephone Nos. 63-2-637-3741 and 631-4446 or
Text 63-917-8537333 or Fax 63-2-637-3731
www.colaycofoundation.com
email: info@colaycofoundation.com